n this changing culture, pastors need
dedication to do what God wants them to
do. They need to hear and heed God's voice.

Most pastors enter ministry to accomplish great things for God's
kingdom. But that drive to make a difference—and the long
hours that result—can crowd out the voice of God. In fact, the
passion to build a church and the passion to know God often turn
out to be mutually exclusive.

In *The Sound of God's Voice,* Roger Barrier writes candidly about
his inability to hear God's voice amid the demands of pastoring—and
describes how he learned to hear God afresh when he dealt with the
thorny issues of pride, spiritual warfare, and personal pain.

*"Roger Barrier writes with honesty and insight about the struggle pastors
face. He speaks from his years of struggle and from his learning along the
way, not from a place of theory. This book moved me to hunger more to
hear and obey the voice of God."*

STEVE SJOGREN
pastor, Vineyard Community Church, author, *Conspiracy of Kind*

Roger Barrier pastors the 6,000 member Casas Adobes B
Church in Tucson, Arizona.

COVER PHOTO: © 2004 LARRY GEDDIS
COVER DESIGN: LeftCoast Design, Portland, OR

US $12.99   Pastora
ISBN 0-8010-9180-2

9 780801 091803   5 1

BakerBooks

THE SOUND
OF GOD'S VOICE

THE SOUND
OF GOD'S VOICE

RECOGNIZING HIS DIRECTION
FOR YOUR MINISTRY

Roger Barrier

BakerBooks

Grand Rapids, Michigan

© 1998 by Roger Barrier

Published by Baker Books
a division of Baker Publishing Group
P.O. Box 6287, Grand Rapids, MI 49516-6287
www.bakerbooks.com

Paperback edition published 2005
ISBN 0-8010-9180-2

Previously published as *Listening to the Voice of God: How Your Ministry Can Be Transformed* in 1998 by Bethany House Publishers

Printed in the United States of America

The Library of Congress has cataloged the hardcover edition as follows:

Barrier, Roger.
    Listening to the voice of God / by Roger Barrier ; David L. Goetz, general editor.
        p.   cm. — (The pastor's soul series)
    ISBN 1-55661-972-3
    1. Clergy—Religious life. 2. Listening—Religious aspects—Christianity.
3. God—Knowableness. 4. Spiritual life—Christianity. I. Goetz, David L.
II. Title. III. Series.
BV4011.6.B37   1998
248.8'92—dc21   00-551016

I dedicate this book to four special people:

To my wife, Julie, for teaching me courage, and for her unwavering inspiration, intimate love, and support;

To my daughter Jessie, who now lives in heaven, for giving me a sense of how much God's heart must ache when baby Christians refuse to grow up;

To my daughter Brianna, for helping me understand the heart of the Father;

To my daughter Bronwyn, for showing me the kind of man I want to become.

Roger Barrier pastors Casas Adobes Baptist Church in Tucson, Arizona. His ministry began in January 1976, just after his graduation from seminary, and he is committed to completing fifty years of pastoral ministry there, God willing. Roger holds degrees from Baylor University, Southwestern Baptist Theological Seminary, and Golden Gate Seminary in Greek, religion, theology, and pastoral care. He and his wife, Julie, are the parents of three daughters.

CONTENTS

ACKNOWLEDGMENTS

EARLY ONE MORNING I peeked into the den to see my dad on his knees in prayer. Instead of bursting into the room with my usual childhood vim and vigor, I stood quietly in the hall and listened as he talked with God. I heard him praying by name for my mom, my brother, and me. I listened as he prayed for his work and business associates. He asked God to strengthen our church and some people who were hurting. When he finished, I turned back down the hall. Somehow, I did not want him to know I had eavesdropped on his talk with God. I was struck by how he and God were just talking. It all sounded so natural.

I suppose there was never a time in my life when I questioned whether or not God interacted in a personal way. I want to thank my mom and dad for raising me in a home where listening for God was as normal and natural as getting up in the morning. When I was a preschooler, Mom sat on my bed and taught me to pray at night. My talking was only a part of the praying. I learned to listen for God to speak back to me. I also want to thank my parents for carefully reading this manuscript and making many helpful suggestions.

As I grew older, I realized that listening for the voice of God could be complex and confusing. For example, God's voice is not the only voice that speaks. I want to thank Albert and Dorothy for taking me under their wings during my teenage years and helping me to sort out how God communicates his will and intentions for life. I especially want to thank Mr. Fox for showing me how to find God's voice in the created universe, and for sharing with me the things God said when it was time for him to die.

Dave and Theresa Ferguson showed me in the Bible how God speaks of a foolproof plan for healing the hurts of both life and the ministry. The plan was there all the time, of course—but I never saw it. I want to thank them for showing me what he said.

I want to thank the church leaders, ministers, and associate pastors from Casas Adobes Baptist Church who have shared with me on many occasions the things they have heard God say. I have learned from them many insights into the "various ways and diverse manners" that God speaks to us today. Especially, I want to thank Gary Shrader for the many times he spoke to me and I recognized immediately that the Lord was speaking directly to me through him. I also thank him for letting me be present when God spoke to him at 6:30 A.M. in that small mountain chapel in Prescott.

I want to thank Ed Rowell for asking me if I ever considered writing a book on pastoral spirituality. I thank him for suggesting me as a person to consider for writing on this topic.

The Thursday afternoon spent at my house with Dave Goetz, discussing the possibility of writing this book, convinced me that there was a book on this subject already bound up inside me. I thank him for helping me get it out. I thank him for his constant encouragement, for his editing expertise, and for helping me understand how to write out of the "overflow of my life."

Most importantly, I thank my wife, Julie, for living side by side with me through all the experiences enumerated here, and for helping me to interpret all that God was saying. I am grateful that she has a sensitive ear to the voice of God. I can always depend on her to help me hear clearly. The life of a pastor's wife can be trying at times. I wish to thank her for standing strong herself and for lifting me up when necessary. She has done double duty for all too long. Thanks.

Finally, I want to thank God for speaking. When I pause to consider all the things that he has going on at any moment throughout the universe, I thrill to think that he takes time to interact and speak with me.

INTRODUCTION

IN EXODUS 20, the people refused Moses' invitation to draw near Mount Sinai and hear God speak. The mountain was shrouded in mist. Thunder roared, and lightning flashed from its heights. The people were afraid.

"Come over and listen to the voice of God," Moses invited.

"No!" they cried out. "We're afraid that if we hear God speak, it will cost us our lives."

Everything changes when God opens his mouth. It is impossible to hear God's voice and remain the same.

We live in a generation that clamors for answers. Now is the time for Christians to speak boldly for God. Too often, though, our flocks are like the folks fleeing Egypt.

"Why don't you go over and hear God," said the people to Moses, "and then come tell us what he said?"

"Now listen, preacher," we seem to hear some say, "I don't want to hear God myself because I have a sneaking suspicion that if I do, he will ask for more than I intend to give. I'm not going as a missionary to

Africa, or going to start tithing, or whatever! So why don't you listen to God, and when I come to church on Sunday, you tell me what God said?"

This book is designed to help pastors hear and identify the voice of God. The first four chapters are intended not only to motivate and inspire us to listen to God but to give practical help on hearing him clearly. The next six chapters take individual topics we face as pastors and give instruction for hearing from God. Of course, the issues we face are many and varied. There is nothing exclusive about the six I have chosen.

Hearing God speak is an exhilarating, intimate, unforgettable, ongoing experience. As we cultivate its art, we inspire our people to understand that the voice of God is nothing to fear. God is to be sought and then welcomed for companionship, comfort, rebuke, guidance, joy, and fulfillment. My prayer is that with a childlike heart of open belief, we can say with the boy Samuel, "Speak, Lord, for your servant is listening."

Roger Barrier
Tucson, Arizona
April 30, 1998

1

DO I REALLY WANT TO HEAR FROM GOD?

I WAS TEACHING PRINCIPLES of spiritual growth in a rented Communist factory auditorium to about one hundred and twenty-five Ukrainian pastors soon after the end of the cold war. The only hotel in the city rented rooms to Ukrainians for $4 per night; it charged Americans $42. The factory cooks prepared our meals for pennies. The daily menu included red borscht, green borscht, and plain borscht.

Each night we all gathered after dinner in a small hotel conference room for impromptu discussions. I was surprised to discover that Ukrainian pastors struggled with many of the same issues pastors encounter in America: "What about spiritual warfare? Can Christians be demon-possessed? How can we organize our people into small groups? How can I find time to prepare good sermons when I already have a full-time job? What is the best way to disciple our people? How can I have a more vibrant prayer life? What about speaking in tongues? Why do Pentecostals and non-Pentecostals fight so much? What about the role of women in the church?"

One night an elderly gentleman, visibly agitated, said, "We've had more experiences with God and suffering than he has [referring to me]. We have been tested by fire. What does he know that we don't know? Why should we listen to him?"

Some were embarrassed by his outburst. Some thought he was right. Every eye was on me.

I turned to the white-haired Ukrainian pastor, who had suffered much during the Communist persecution, and said, "You don't understand how humbling it is for me to presume to teach anything to you. I've walked through your cemeteries and seen thousands of tree-stump-shaped tombstones (which symbolize lives cut off before their time) with death dates all ending in 1931. I know Stalin sold your grain to Germany that year to raise cash and that five million Ukrainians starved. I saw thousands of grave markers dated 1941 and 1942. I know the German invasion and harsh winter killed millions in those two years. I can't comprehend your suffering.

"Twenty years ago I read *The Gulag Archipelago* and *One Day in the Life of Ivan Denisovich* by Aleksandr Solzhenitsyn, and God put it in my heart then to pray for you."

When I mentioned those books, the atmosphere in the room changed. I slowly proceeded, "I am overwhelmed, after years of praying for your strength, protection, safety, and courage, to be here as your teacher. May I sit quietly at your feet and learn from you for a while? You tell me your stories."

So they did. Some had torture scars. Several told of the sufferings and deaths of loved ones. One young air force lieutenant told of a recent confrontation with soldiers in his squadron who demanded either his renunciation of Christ or his death by their hands. These people had experienced the fellowship of sharing in Christ's sufferings. They knew the cost of following Jesus. That night I decided to begin my next morning's session with a question about what it might cost to hear God speak.

The next day I said, "How many of you want to hear God speak?" Every hand was raised. I asked them a second question: "Have you ever wondered why there are so few prophets in the Bible?" I paused to let the query sink in; then I paraphrased several biblical scenarios:

God said to Hosea, "Do you want to hear me speak?"

"I would love to be your prophet."

"Then go marry a prostitute."

"But God, I am a preacher. I can't marry her. She will ruin my ministry."

The truth is, she made his ministry, but hearing God speak cost him a lot. She broke his heart.

Then one day God asked Jeremiah, "Do you want to hear me speak?"

"God, I'm too young to be a prophet, but the truth is, I'd love to hear you speak."

So God spoke to Jeremiah. People cursed him, mocked him, tossed him in jail, and bound him in chains. They threw him in cisterns and beat him senseless. They humiliated him in stocks in the marketplaces. Was hearing God speak worth it? The people never believed a word Jeremiah said.

One day God commanded Isaiah, "Take off your clothes."

"Why?"

"Don't ask me why. Just take them off."

"Well, for how long?"

"Until I tell you to put them on again."

So Isaiah took off his clothes. Imagine the scene as he walked naked down the streets of Jerusalem.

"Hey, Isaiah," asked the people, "where are your clothes?"

"I took them off."

"Why?"

Imagine the looks when he said, "Well, I heard this little voice . . ."

Finally, three years later, God again spoke. "Isaiah, put on your clothes and pronounce this word from the Lord to the people: 'As I have bared your buttocks, so I will bare the buttocks of Egypt and spank them.'"

At this point I looked into the faces of men and women who knew how to suffer for Christ. I asked again: "Now, how many of you want to hear God speak?" Not a hand went up. I waited quietly. Then one hand raised uncertainly—and then another—but no more.

I continued, "I intend to teach on *how* to hear God speak. Shall we proceed?" Every hand in the room went up. Even those who knew suffering had hesitated at the cost of hearing God speak.

Listening price

In Exodus 20, the Israelites refused Moses' invitation to come to the base of the mountain and hear God speak. Their excuse sounds remarkably up-to-date.

"No," they said. "We are afraid that if we hear the voice of God, it will cost us our lives."

Hearing from God precludes the possibility that we can remain the same. The *want to* issue of hearing God speak must be settled before the *how to* part can draw us close to God.

After pastoring the same church for more than twenty years, I was worn out, exhausted. Our church faced relocation to a new site and reorganization of the entire staff as growth and cultural changes brought increasing demands. I pleaded with God to move me to another place. I told God I would go any-where—I just wanted a fresh start in a place where I could recycle my sermons and preach twenty-plus-years' worth of church-member stories that I dared not use in the church where they occurred. In short, I wanted out.

I went to bed one night knowing there would be little sleep as I wrestled with the problems at hand. Sure enough, at 3:00 A.M. I was wide-awake. As I walked down the hall to the bathroom, I sensed God draw near: *Roger, I'm not going to move you. I have plans for you here. Your work is not finished. Let's meet on the couch now and talk this over.*

I wanted to hear God but had no intention of meeting with God on the couch to hear his reasons for keeping me in the pressure cooker. Disappointed, I went back to bed.

In the morning I apologized to God for my behavior. If he wanted me at Casas Adobes Baptist Church until retirement, I would fulfill his will. I asked God to strengthen me with the power of Jesus Christ, based on Philippians 4:10–13, and to help me be content and victorious in my present situation.

It is hard to want to listen to God when I sense he intends to say things I don't want to hear.

Hesitating instincts

Through the years other reasons have caused me to hesitate to come to the foot of the mountain and listen to the voice of God. One reason was because I had been burned in the past. One evening I was sitting beside my fiancée in a little church we occasionally attended during college. Shortly before the service began, a woman spoke quietly to Julie.

"I have a word from the Lord for you," she said. "You will be like the prophetess Anna in Luke 2. You will be widowed after seven years and spend the rest of your life ministering in sweet service to God."

My first instinct was to tell the intruder I doubted

God told her anything—that she had imagined it. If God had something to tell Julie, he was perfectly capable of telling her himself, but I held my tongue and looked at the young girl who would soon be my wife.

I hate to admit that I worried occasionally during the first seven years of our marriage. On the evening of our eighth anniversary, I intentionally stayed awake until midnight. As I stood in the bathroom, I finally knew that woman's dismal forebodings were nothing more than a figment of her misguided imagination.

Another reason why I hesitated to listen to God's voice was that, frankly, I didn't know how. The seminary I attended required approximately thirty classes for a Master of Divinity degree. As I recall, not a single class explained how to hear God speak. Looking back, I see that my seminary experience was focused on becoming biblically smart and ministerially efficient. Cultivating the spiritual life was an afterthought.

Plus, there are many competing voices about how or if God speaks: Some Roman Catholics say, "Do it like this." Some Pentecostals say, "No, do it like this." Some northern Reformed evangelicals say, "This is how you do it." Some dispensationalists say, "God does not do it."

And how can I be certain whether I heard from God, from Satan, or from myself?

Most pastors admit to times when God spoke uniquely to them. When I ask them to explain how they knew it was God, they respond something like this: "I had this impression deep down inside."

ROGER BARRIER

"But how do you know it was God?"

"I just know."

Where God speaks and how God speaks may be hard to quantify and hard to explain. Sometimes, confirming the voice of God is easy. The first time I knew God spoke to me was when I was seven years old. During a Wednesday evening prayer meeting, I heard the laypreacher say something about shepherds and sheep. As I put down my coloring book to pull another crayon out of the box, I sensed a quiet voice deep within: *Roger, you are a lost sheep.* At home later that evening, I asked my parents, "I am a lost sheep, aren't I?" I did not know what a "sheep" was or what "lost" meant. By Saturday morning my conversion was solidly in place.

Two weeks later I again heard God speak. I was sitting in church on Sunday night, and while our pastor preached, I had an overwhelming impression God was near: *When you grow up, I want you to be a preacher.* I remember turning to see who was speaking. No one was there. I believe God was communicating deep in my "knower," giving direction to my life. (I call the place where God speaks to me my "knower." In chapter 3, I identify this descriptive term with the biblical concept of the human spirit. My clarification goes something like this: "I'm not certain I can put this into words, but there's this place deep inside where I know God speaks. I call it my 'knower,' and it is there that I have heard the voice of God." When I explain

24

this to pastors, I often see a knowing grin and a nodding agreement.)

Satan speaks, self speaks, and God speaks—and sometimes I cannot distinguish among the three. Because of this, I feared losing credibility. If I announced what I thought God told me, only to discover later that I was wrong, I would only embarrass myself. Occasionally older Christians have told me that God promised them they would live to see the glorious return of Christ. I have conducted the funerals of most of those folks. Obviously, they mistook something else for the voice of God.

Several years ago we considered relocating our church operations. Standing in front of the bathroom mirror one Saturday, I almost dropped my razor at the thought that flashed into my mind. Instead of going through all the trouble and expense of relocating, why not purchase the eight houses surrounding our property? We could build a new worship center and expand our parking lots, making room for growth. I thanked God for revealing this new course of action.

I told our church leaders what God told me, and we made plans to purchase the adjoining houses. Selling prices were negotiated and contracts signed. The subdivision deed restrictions required that a majority of the 156 nearby homeowners agree with the sale and rezoning. Six months, numerous unpleasant neighborhood association meetings, and more than one hundred irate neighbors later, we called off the deal. I was still licking my wounds when a wise saint put everything in perspective.

"God spoke about this issue long ago," she said, "in one of the Ten Commandments. Remember? 'Thou shalt not covet thy neighbor's house.'"

My credibility—not God's—is on the line when I boldly announce what I think he might have said. No wonder I hesitate to listen for God's voice.

Where God leads

As my relationship with God matured, I decided it was better to risk a few mistakes than to give up. I decided I wanted to hear God speak—at any price! Any other conclusion seemed incongruous with pastoral ministry.

One Friday night the phone rang in my bedroom less than an hour before I was to conduct a wedding rehearsal.

"I just heard that Dick and Jane are getting married tomorrow in your church," said a close pastor friend from across town. "Are you performing the service?"

"Yes."

"Did you know that they are under discipline from our church for issues regarding their previous marriages? We refused to marry them until they sorted out the issues they raised in our church. So they went over to your church to get married. I appeal to you as a Christian brother not to perform a wedding we refused to perform. Please respect our church's position. We Christians in this community must be unified in our actions and support one another."

I was stunned. But God had already told me what to do. While my friend was on the phone, I had a deep impression from God to do whatever my friend requested.

"Give me a few minutes to pray," I said, "and I will call you right back."

I got on my knees in the bedroom and asked God to confirm what I thought he had said. Deep in my "knower," I knew God was telling me not to perform the wedding. However, this was not at all what I wanted to hear. The wedding was scheduled; the guests were invited; the musicians and vocalists were arranged; the flowers were purchased; the cakes were baked; and the honeymoon was set.

How could I not conduct the wedding? They would be embarrassed; I would be embarrassed. I called back my friend.

"I'll honor your request." I said, "However, I have one of my own. Would you approve of the wedding if the couple can meet with you and your church leaders before tomorrow afternoon and settle out the discipline issues?"

"There is no way we can settle the issues so quickly," he said. "But if they want to, I will get our people together in the morning and meet with them. We'll see what happens."

I conducted the rehearsal as planned. Before the

rehearsal dinner, I spent a moment in private with the bride and groom, relaying the content of the call. I was the one surprised; they had expected my pastor friend would call.

"If you are willing, we will meet here at the church with their leaders and try to iron this out in the morning," I said. "If you settle with them, I will be glad to marry you at 1:00 P.M., as scheduled. Otherwise, I cannot."

For more than four hours, the couple met with their pastor and church leaders. By noon it finally dawned on me there would be no wedding. By 1:15 the guests had arrived, the music was playing, and everyone was discussing the whereabouts of the pastor and the bride and groom. I was sitting in a chair in my jeans and sport shirt, observing the drawn-out discussion. The bride and groom were not happy.

"I suppose I had better tell folks there will be no wedding today," I said. I made my way to the sanctuary and stood at the altar.

"Dick and Jane have discovered some issues they need to work on before they proceed with their wedding," I began. "So we have agreed to call off the wedding to sort out the issues. The food is prepared for the reception, and the bride and groom have decided that since we are all here, we might as well enjoy the fellowship. Let me pray for Dick and Jane, and then we will dismiss to the fellowship hall."

Dick and Jane I hardly knew, their friends not at all. But friend after friend approached me quietly at the reception to commend what I had done. Again and again people said, "This needed to happen."

That weekend took a lot out of me. I took no pleasure in my actions, or from the plight of the bridal pair, but only from knowing I had obeyed God.

2

THE POWER OF A CLEAN HEART

I STEPPED INTO THE COOL, humid October night. The air was frosty and my breath condensed like exhaled smoke. It was one of those nights when car defrosters labor to keep condensation off the glass. Eight children clamored into my car, and I led a six-car procession of church members away from the Hillsboro skating rink and down the highway toward Penelope—population: 226—and the small country church I pastored during my college years. Three or four blocks later, I noticed dimly flashing lights through my fogged-over rear windshield.

Instinctively I checked the speedometer. "I'm not speeding; what could be wrong?" The entire procession pulled over with me and waited while the police officer approached my car. I got out and innocently asked, "What's wrong, officer?"

"Didn't you see that stop sign?"

"Stop sign? What stop sign?" I looked back into the gloom. There it was. "I'm sorry; I didn't see it."

"Maybe the reason you didn't see it was because you were driving with your lights off."

"Driving with my lights off?"

I reached into the car, pulled the knob, and on came the lights. I was incredulous!

Then the officer said, "Maybe the reason you didn't notice your lights were off was because your windows were fogged over."

He continued, "Maybe that was because the children were making quite a commotion. Do you know that the legal limit for occupants in a car in the state of Texas is eight? I count nine in there including you."

The police officer stepped out on the road and motioned the waiting church members to get on with their journey. I avoided eye contact as my passing flock strained for a better look at their shepherd. When they were gone, the officer said sternly, "Son, I have enough to run you into the Hillsboro county jail. But I am going to give you a break. You get in your car, clean off those windows, silence those children, and drive straight out of town. If I catch you in Hillsboro again tonight, I'll throw you in jail. Now go."

I got in the car, dried off the windshield, told the children to be quiet, and drove in humiliation back to Penelope to face my waiting parishioners. How could I have been so careless? It did not take much reflection to answer that question. There was so much confusion in my car—children yelling, windows fogging—I didn't notice that I was driving in the dark.

Several years later, as I was reading the sixth Beatitude—"Blessed are the pure in heart, for they shall see God"—I finally understood the spiritual implication of the police stop. A dirty, clogged-up heart impairs my ability to see and hear God just as much as a commotion-filled car with fogged-over windows and no lights makes it impossible to see a stop sign in the night.

There are times in my life when it seems God is silent. I know that God sometimes hides himself for spiritual reasons, remaining quiet for a season. But more often than not, the reason I do not hear from God has less to do with his inscrutable purposes than with the fact that I live with a fogged-over, dirtied-up spirit. Only the pure in heart see God. He loves to prompt, communicate with, and lead us, but sin impairs our ability to hear him.

Sins of the spirit

Pick a sin, any sin. I'll start with pride, which is one of the hidden sins of ministry. I can talk with feeling about how I desire to reach people and grow a church for the glory of God, never realizing I have mixed self-image needs and personal ambitions into the equation. Pride is deceptive and easy to miss, and since God does not share his glory, pride can bring unimagined hindrances to a ministry.

I knew a pastor who initiated a church plant in the suburbs of a major city. The cover of his slick, four-color brochure, designed to arouse community awareness, was adorned with the penetrating announcement: "He is coming." The arrangement of the cover art and wording implied that no less a personage than Jesus Christ himself was on the way. As I held the brochure I pondered the improbable. *Surely, I would turn the page and see a picture of the Lord Jesus.* I opened the brochure, and there he was—only *he* didn't look much like Jesus. That may seem innocent enough, except that this man was known for his penchant for publicity.

Overt manifestations of pride—when I want to be seen out in front, or when I love to have my name mentioned in public—are easy to identify. But pride can be more subtle. For years I struggled with shyness. I was afraid to be myself because I feared what people might think. I never considered my shyness to be a manifestation of pride until a wise saint pointed out that pride is simply an overconcern with self. Suddenly I realized my shyness and fear of displeasing people were not unfortunate personality traits; they were evidence of pride—an overconcerned focus on *myself.* I discuss this sin more fully in a later chapter.

Another sin is bitterness. The apostle Paul indicates that a spirit of bitterness gives Satan a foothold. As a pastor, I have enough battles to fight without opening a door to Satan. Yet the opportunities to be slighted, criticized, and hurt arise in ministry all too often. When I get hurt, I tend to get angry. When I fail to properly handle the anger, I soon nurse a spirit of bitterness. Eventually, my bitterness sours relationships, generates cynicism, and dirties my inner spirit.

Several years ago I welcomed into our fellowship a man who had been twice-burned in ministry. We helped him heal and entrusted him with a Sunday morning adult Bible class. About a year later several

church members warned me that he was quietly discussing the possibility of leading a group out of our
church and starting his own church. Since I had
invested many hours in him, I put little stock in the
warnings. However, weeks later, in a gesture of grace
and compassion, I stood before more than one hundred of my parishioners and gave my blessing to their
departure.

"Are you angry?" people asked.

"Oh no," I replied, as I inwardly seethed. The newly
self-proclaimed pastor wrote me nice letters of grati-
tude and encouragement. He told me God often laid
it on his heart to pray for me. I never responded to his
letters.

Several years later my wife and I were evaluating
our spiritual lives. Julie said, "You and God are not
very close right now, are you."

"No, everything's fine. Our relationship has never
been better."

"That's not what I see. While praying recently, I
sensed God telling me that you are harboring a spirit
of bitterness against _____ (she named the man
who had started the new church). Your spiritual life
will go nowhere until you restore that relationship.
You need to respond—and forgive him."

My defenses melted.

Another sin is envy, which is a constant temptation for pastors. I often see people in our church buy-
ing things and doing things that I wish I could buy or
do. Our high school minister grieved over the tradi-

tionally low pay in the ministry. "I know our church tries hard to be competitive," he said, "but I could make more in the secular world." Another time he said, "I accept lower pay as part of the ministry, but it hurts when I see our church youth with new clothes and new cars, and I can't afford to buy all that stuff for my kids." He paused thoughtfully, then said angrily, "And you know what really ticks me off? Most of those things were bought with money that should have been their tithe—I can just feel it!" Many pastors can identify with his frustration.

Still another sin is the spirit of selfish competition. I find myself comparing my church with other churches, forgetting that we are all on the same team and working for the same God. I occasionally find myself wanting to outdo the churches down the street or in another city. But the spirit of competition saps joy from ministry and hinders my effectiveness before God.

One Sunday I opened the door to the choir room and found a yellow poster taped to the glass: "Musicians needed for a new church start! Come be a part of our new church family." I could not believe it—the nerve of proselytizing brazenly right in our choir room! Angrily, I pulled the poster from the door but had second thoughts as I walked down the hallway. *We have plenty of musicians*, I thought. *Surely we would not miss a few who wanted to help out another church. They would have more opportunities to use their gifts regularly there than in our church, anyway.*

When I passed another yellow poster at the end of the hall, I left it there.

Not only can sin fog-over our spirit, so can good things. During the week I prepare sermons, read my Bible, counsel the troubled, perform weddings, officiate at funerals, raise my children, love my wife, play golf, read for pleasure, develop relationships, lead the church, balance the checkbook, phone my parents, spend time with my in-laws, mow the grass, participate in a small group, ride my bike, and shop at the mall. Pastors lead busy lives. Near the end of the week it dawns on me that I have not heard from God. When I look inside my spirit where the Holy Spirit resides, I find sermons, Bible studies, needy people, weddings, funerals, children, my wife, golf, novels, friends, the church, my finances, my mom and dad, my in-laws, the lawn, my small group, my bike, and the mall.

Where's God?

Then once again I remind myself to take time for God, reduce the number of my activities, and cultivate the art of hearing from God.

Restoring the fellowship

Late one evening, after my third-born had gotten out of bed for what seemed like the hundredth time, I lost my temper. I yelled at Bronwyn to get back into bed, and she wept as she scampered away. About 10:00 P.M. my wife finally came home from choir practice.

Bronwyn called from the back of the house, "Is

that Mom? I want to see Mom!" Mom was home all right, but it was late, and Bronwyn should have been asleep hours ago; and besides, I wanted some time with Mom. So I yelled back, "No. Mom's not home yet. Go to sleep."

Moments later, her little face peered into the room: "Dad, why did you lie to me?"

I did what any good parent would do—I sent her straight to bed.

Our fellowship was broken that night—but not our relationship. The father-daughter relationship hadn't changed, but the father-daughter *fellowship* was impaired. I was miserable, and I knew she was miserable. Early the next morning, I sat on her bed and apologized: "I am sorry. I was wrong. I don't lie to you often, but I did last night, and I apologize. Please forgive me."

She put her arms around my neck and said, "Okay, I forgive you. You're the best dad in the whole world."

Confession is the God-given tool for restoring fellowship. Most of us *know* how to restore fellowship with God—we preach about it often. But the actual restoration can be difficult. I find I must make a concentrated effort to restore broken fellowship or I can muddle on in my interactions with God for weeks, even years. John writes, "If we confess our sins, he is faithful and just and will forgive us our sins and purify us from all unrighteousness" (1 John 1:9).

I've discovered that my fellowship with God is restored when my confession is specific. When I was a boy, I had numerous chores such as mowing the grass and taking out the trash. I occasionally made my bed and washed the dishes, but my mother always did the laundry. When I left for college, she sewed a canvas duffel bag for me and said, "Put your dirty clothes in the bag every night. At the end of the week, go to the Laundromat and wash your clothes."

Seven days later I took the duffel bag filled with my dirty clothes to the coin-operated Laundromat down the street. I thought I'd save a little time, so I threw the bag in the washer, put in some laundry powder, inserted the proper change, and turned on the machine. Moments later a loud "thump, thump, thump, thump, thump" echoed through the Laundromat. A pretty Baylor co-ed approached with a grin: "I watched you load your washer. I think the clothes would get cleaner if you took them out of the bag."

One day, when my relationship with God was hurting, I remembered my experience in the Laundromat. My usual prayer of confession went something like "Dear God, please forgive me for all the sins I have committed today." Suddenly I realized that my confession model was about as effective in cleansing my sins as my first laundry experience was at cleaning my clothes. No wonder my relationship with God was struggling. Each sin needs individual attention.

Today my confession model is simple. When I realize I have sinned, I detail to God what I have done and then say, "I agree with you that what I did was wrong." I ask God to forgive me, and then affirm my intention never to commit that sin again. I pray on a regular basis the prayer in Psalm 139: "Search me, O God, and know my heart; test me and know my anxious thoughts. See if there is any offensive way in me, and lead me in the way everlasting" (vv. 23–24).

I wait quietly for God to bring unconfessed sin to my attention. The Holy Spirit is very specific: "At four P.M. last Tuesday, Roger, you did this and this and this."

I was near the end of a morning jog, when God brought to mind a sin I committed when I was a teenager. Immediately my face flushed red and felt hot. I felt foolish as I looked around and realized no one was near to observe my reaction. I confessed that sin and asked God for forgiveness. About a half hour later I was in the shower debriefing the experience when I realized I could not remember the sin that brought on the embarrassed blush—so completely had God removed it. If God brings nothing to mind when I pray Psalm 139, I don't worry about what I cannot remember. However, when he does, I deal with it immediately.

Every day I live with unconfessed sin is a day my ability to hear God is impaired. Occasionally I ask myself, *When was the last time I heard God speak?* Then I consider, *When was the last time I carefully confessed my sins?* The two answers are closely related.

Confession is essential to maintaining the intimate fellowship conducive to hearing the inner voice of God.

Blinded by the glory

The sun was peeking over the horizon as I jogged along a deserted Arizona road. Somewhere out in the desert, with not a car in sight and several miles from my house, I offered up a prayer, "Just once, God, I'd like to see your glory. I want to be like Moses the day you let him see your glory!"

Immediately I apologized to God for my arrogance.

Then I thought, *I'm no Moses, but I'd like to see God. Why can't I pray to see God's glory?* I lifted my hands and prayed, "Dear God, I want to see your glory before I die. In fact, I want to see you like Isaiah saw you in the temple—high and mighty and lifted up." I turned for home and considered how God often manifested his glory as light.

Six months later I was preaching in our sanctuary when a teenage boy, fifteen rows back on the left, pulled out a flashlight and held it near his belt buckle. I recognized it as a long, round, cylindrical model that held eight or ten D-size batteries. Moments later he aimed it at my face and switched it on. I paused in my sermon, and said, "Please turn off the flashlight." He turned it off.

Ten minutes later he did it again. I was surprised by the power of the light. My irises closed down. I had trouble adjusting to the darkened page of my sermon notes. I blinked my eyes, lifted my hand, and pointed my finger directly at him: "Son, I can't see! Would you please stop shining that flashlight in my face?" He switched it off again.

I was hot with anger.

Worship services at Casas dismiss with the congregation singing a song after the sermon—but not this Sunday! I asked one of our elders to pray a dismissal prayer, and while every head was bowed, I walked quickly down the aisle. When the elder said, "Amen," I was standing face-to-face with my adversary. I accosted him immediately: "I didn't appreciate your shining that flashlight in my face."

He looked at me quizzically: "What flashlight?"

"You know what I'm talking about! The one you held at your belt buckle and kept shining in my face during the sermon."

"I don't have a flashlight."

I was incredulous. "Of course you do. I saw you holding it at your belt buckle."

"I don't have a flashlight!"

I knew he was lying, so I did the only thing that made sense. "May I frisk you?" I asked.

He was so startled that he lifted his arms. By now a crowd had gathered. It is not often that a pastor confronts a teenager in the pew after church—especially an eighteen-year-old high school football lineman. He was an imposing sight as he stood with arms outstretched.

His mother and father were incensed. Their son was not a Christian; his parents had brought him to church for years hoping he would come to know

Christ. All their prayers and long talks were in jeopardy as I accused their son while church people gathered round. Now *they* were hot with anger.

But I didn't care about any of that. I wanted to see the flashlight. All I knew about frisking I'd learned on television—I patted around his chest, under his armpits, and down his back. There was no need to go further. I had made a serious mistake. I furtively glanced under the pew. But there was no flashlight there either. I was dumbfounded.

I could not apologize enough. The young man smiled and told me to forget it. "No big deal," he said.

My relationship with his mom and dad was estranged until a year later when his dad called to relate a remarkable experience.

"I have something you need to hear," he said. "Last night I got the one-thirty A.M. phone call all parents dread—'Dad, I'm over at my girlfriend's apartment. Can you come over right now and talk with us?'

"My imagination ran wild: Was she pregnant? Were they going to get married?

"I was totally unprepared for what happened when I arrived at the apartment. My son opened the door and said, 'Dad, my girlfriend and I want you to explain how we can become Christians.' I gathered my composure and knelt with them by the living room couch and led them both to a saving knowledge of Jesus Christ.

"Later I asked him what had changed his mind about Christ. He replied, 'Well, I'd been talking with my cousin, and he encouraged me to give my life to Christ. I'd been thinking about it. But what really got my attention was last year when Roger accused me of shining that flashlight in his face. You didn't know it, Dad, but I lay in bed the night before and made a bargain with God. I told him I would follow Christ if he proved to me that he was real. I proposed a test. I told God I would listen carefully to Roger's sermon the next morning, and if I could find three things that directly applied to me, I would know he was real and would surrender my life to him. On the other hand, if I could not find three things, I would never go to church again. I listened carefully to the sermon and found two points that sort of applied to me. When the sermon was over, I was disappointed. Have you noticed, Dad, I have not been to church since that day?

"'Tonight it dawned on me: God did answer my prayer. Remember about ten minutes into the sermon, when Roger looked at me and told me to turn off the flashlight? Then, about ten minutes later, he pointed his finger directly at me and said, "Son, would you please stop shining that flashlight in my face? I can't see!" Finally, at the close of the service, Roger accused me face-to-face. Three times he spoke directly to me. Dad, Roger hasn't spoken ten words to me in the nine years we've gone to that church. God passed the test. He is real.'"

After I hung up the phone, I paused to debrief: I'd asked to see God's glory, and, when he answered, I mistook the light of his glory for a flashlight. At choir practice later that week, I asked if anyone in the choir loft had seen "the light." They all remembered my pointing to the boy and talking about the flashlight, but no one actually saw what I saw.

Then again, I was the only one who had prayed to see God's glory.

My faith strengthened and my resolve to listen to God increased. I want to keep my spirit clean at all costs; not only do I want to be able to hear God's voice, I never want to miss seeing his glory. The best reason not to sin—and to confess it when I do—is because only the pure in heart will hear and see God.

3

THE SOUND OF GOD'S VOICE

THE VOICE ON THE PHONE was not unfamiliar. She announced she had a message for me from God. I, as well as others, had heard her claim to be a prophetess. Since that gift is not emphasized in our congregation, and because of some unusual quirks of her personality, I considered her one of God's strange people who occasionally flow through a church family.

Without pausing to inquire if I were interested, she launched into a detailed pronouncement that my wife, Julie, and I would soon suffer a divorce. I had neglected my wife, she said, and failed to build the kind of marriage relationship God intended for pastors. The penalty would be the forfeiture of my marriage.

I knew enough not to laugh out loud or question her sanity or tell her what she could do with her message. I thanked her for calling and hung up.

Could God really be speaking through her? What if she were right? Does God still speak through prophets and prophetesses today? What would they sound like if he did? Would he ever choose someone like her?

The pages of Scripture are filled with stories of unusual people who did strange things under the guise of "Thus saith the Lord." But there was some truth in what she said. What pastor ever spends enough time with his family? Julie and I talked often about the sacrifices of ministry—not the least of which were the sacrifices we made in our marriage. We knew that when outside pressures demanded our full attention, we could put our marriage on hold for weeks at a time, knowing the immediate pressures would not last forever. When things settled down, a few days of conscious recovery brought quick healing and restoration.

Nevertheless, few marriages are strong enough to withstand many of those times without some damage. Had we put things on hold once too often? Was God now upset and getting personally involved? Surely not. I placed a call to one of my spiritual advisers.

"Charles, I need your advice," I said. "I'm 99 percent sure her message was not from God. But help me verify for certain so I can move on to something else. I don't want to sit around worrying about this."

"When God warned of doom in the Bible," he said, "he usually provided a means for avoiding the consequences—often by repentance and/or restitution. Did the warning give any hope for reconciling the marriage and avoiding the divorce?"

"No."

"Then the message was not from God."

How does a person know whether he or she really heard from God?

While God speaks in many ways, he provides an internal spiritual organ known as the human spirit that, when properly cultivated, is dependable in hearing God speak. In *Faith—Tried and Triumphant*,[1] D. Martin Lloyd-Jones wrote about various ways God communicates, and then he described a more mystical approach:

> Then God sometimes answers directly in our spirit. The prophet said, "I will watch and see what he will say in me." God speaks to me by speaking in me. He can so lay something upon the mind that we are certain of the answer. He can impress something upon our spirits in an unmistakable manner. We find ourselves unable to get away from an impression that is on our mind or heart; we try to rid ourselves of it, but back it comes. So does God answer at times.

I believe there is nothing mystical about the Holy Spirit's speaking to my human spirit. In fact, I believe this is the most normal and consistent means by which God communicates. Shortly after graduating from seminary, my wife, Julie, and I prayed for an opportunity to pastor in a place with many non-Christians and not many churches. Since there were more than thirty-five churches within a three-mile radius of my home church in Dallas, we sensed we were needed elsewhere. One Sunday afternoon the phone rang as I was

---

[1] D. Martin Lloyd-Jones, *Faith—Tried and Triumphant* (Grand Rapids, Mich.: Baker Book House, 1994), 30.

leaving to fly to Denver to candidate at a church. The caller was from Tucson: "We have your résumé. Would you fly out and interview with our church next week?" she asked.

We talked for several moments until I had to excuse myself. I had to catch the plane to Denver.

While talking on the phone with Doris, I felt God tell me I would become pastor of that church in Tucson. I hung up and turned to Julie: "I'm going on to Denver, but God just told me we're going to pastor in Tucson."

Julie smiled, "I know. While you were talking, he told me the same thing."

A week later Julie and I were on a plane to Tucson, and we have served that church for more than twenty years with never a doubt that it was the place to which God had called us.

People sometimes ask, "How did you know for sure Tucson was where God wanted you?"

I don't try to explain all about the human soul and spirit. I usually say, "Have you ever had the experience where deep down inside you just knew what to do— where God gives you impressions, encouragement, and advice?" I see a light of recognition in their eyes.

Then I continue, "I call that place my 'knower.' Down deep in my 'knower,' I knew what God wanted."

The Bible term for "knower" is the "human spirit." I have discovered that God delights to communicate with me deep in my spirit.

I have learned to be careful when listening for the

voice of God. His is not the only voice that speaks. I don't want to be misled by my imagination, and I certainly do not care to be fooled by Satan's temptations, accusations, or deceits. Whenever I sense what may be a word from God, I refuse to accept it until I carefully consider whether I am hearing from God, myself, or Satan. My overriding principle is simple: I don't do anything until I am certain who is speaking.

Over the years I have developed a checklist of what I think God's voice sounds like. The following list paints in broad strokes and is certainly not complete or foolproof. No one point is sufficient to prove the voice of God.

1. *God speaks in my innermost spirit. Satan and I speak in my soul or human mind.* As I mature spiritually, my increasing spiritual experience and discernment allow me to distinguish better between my soul and my spirit. My understanding is that God himself takes up residence deep in my inner spirit during conversion. There he lives and speaks. Self and Satan have access to my mind, but God alone has access to my innermost human spirit. Following the guidelines of Hebrews 4:12, I quiet my mind and allow the Word of God to divide between soul and spirit. As I listen for God to speak deep within, I try to discern whether what I hear emanates from my soul (my mind) or from my inner human spirit.

What originates from my mind, I take to be from either self or Satan. What comes from deep in my inner spirit can only be from God. I do not take this first guideline lightly or flippantly. Discerning between soul and spirit requires patience, practice, and careful cultivation.

2. God tends to speak with gentle leadings. Remember how God spoke to Elijah? He was not in the swirling wind, the violent earthquake, or the raging fire. When all was still, God spoke with a gentle whisper (1 Kings 19:11–13).

I remember being pressured by a pushy used-car salesman to buy a car I really wanted. He told me, "I have another couple who want this car, too. They are trying to arrange financing right now. They could return at any minute. If you want this car, you need to make an offer quickly."

Not liking that kind of pressure, I turned my back and calmly walked away.

My experience is that God seldom pushes and drives and demands like an aggressive, assertive used-car salesman. The Word of God is open to reason. God seldom urges sudden action without giving us time to think through the issues. I try to differentiate between the promptings of God and my drive to fulfill my hurried agenda.

3. God's voice produces freedom. In Matthew 11:30, Jesus says, "My yoke is easy and my burden is light." I was sitting high up on Skyline Drive overlooking the city of Tucson one evening, when I felt an overwhelming burden to reach the city for Christ. I used to pray for big burdens like that—but not anymore. Our city needs to be reached for Christ, but God has called many pastors to share in the work. If I am not careful, I can feel frustrated by biting off more ministry than God intends for me to chew.

I have known pastors whose burdened attitudes for some community or group are more hindrance than help. They live so full of guilt that no one wants to be around them. Satan loves to put people into bondage; God loves to set them free.

4. God tends to speak when I am seeking him. Jeremiah reported God as saying: "Then you will call upon me and come and pray to me, and I will listen to you. You will seek me and find me when you seek me with all your heart" (Jer. 29:12–13).

After the first three months, the church I was newly pastoring filled to capacity. We had space problems and no clear options. I was getting ready to preach one Sunday when the answer came. I walked to the pulpit, and on the spur of the moment I announced that God had just told me the answer to our overcrowded worship problems. He wanted us to remodel our fellowship hall into worship space. At the close of the service, the deacon who oversaw construction of both our worship chapel and fellowship hall handed me a tape measure from the back of his truck.

"Here, I'll loan you this for a week," he said. "Why don't you measure and see if God is really the one behind your proposal." He winked as he left.

So I measured the fellowship hall and discovered that it was only two feet wider and four feet longer than the chapel—hardly enough room to make remodeling worthwhile. The next Sunday I walked to the pulpit and informed the people that God had changed his mind. Everybody had a good laugh, and I learned a lesson. Both self and Satan may inject thoughts and impressions into my mind when I'm not consciously seeking God. Both tend to speak with sudden intrusions of thoughts into the mind. But God's voice is heard when I diligently listen for it.

5. When God is speaking, there is a sense that everything is under control. God wants us in control of our faculties and decisions. God related that "the spirits of prophets are subject to the control of prophets"(1 Cor. 14:32). Paul warns that Satan wants to ensnare and control people when he speaks in 2 Timothy 2:24–26 of the hope that "they will come to their senses and escape from the trap of the devil, who has taken them captive to do his will." When self and Satan speak, there is an inner sense that something is out of control.

6. God gives specific directions. In my pastoral role, people often approach me for help in discerning God's will. Many times I sense God has already told them his intentions. I do not hesitate to ask, "God's already told you exactly what to do, hasn't he?" Many times they smile and nod sheepishly. I clarify some of the specifics and do my best to ascertain that there are no hidden issues or agendas. Then I encourage them to proceed with what they have heard.

On other occasions, people feel confused when they share what they think God said. "Then don't do anything at all," I say. "If you are not certain, either God has not spoken or you have not heard clearly. God is not the author of confusion." Satan and self, however, often communicate in confused, uncertain wonderings. But when God speaks, there is no doubt about what to do.

7. God convicts of specific sins. John 16:8 teaches that the Holy Spirit "will convict the world of guilt in regard to sin and righteousness and judgment." My experience is that when God convicts of sin, his voice is quite specific: *Yesterday at two* P.M. *you did this.* I know exactly what I did and when I did it.

Satan and self, on the other hand, often accuse in broad generalities, leaving me with an unfocused sense of haunting guilt centered around poor choices, questioned priorities, unfinished responsibilities, or unmet expectations. It took years in the ministry before I figured this out. Now when I feel accused or have a nagging sense of unspecified guilt, I pause and consider why I feel so guilty. If there is not a definite sense of conviction about a specific sin, I know the feelings are not from God's Spirit. They emanate from the "accuser of our brothers" (Revelation 12:10)—or from other internal, personal issues that need attention.

8. *God speaks with 100 percent truth that can be tested by the Word of God.* Once a young woman related to me how God had led her to plan marriage with a man who was not a Christian. When I pointed out in the Bible that God said Christians were not to be unequally yoked to unbelievers, she responded, "But I know God spoke to me and told me to marry him." She was unimpressed when I reasoned with her that God would not say one thing in the Bible and another to her. The voice we hear inside is always open for testing and comparison with the truths of the Bible. Satan and self often traffic in lies, deceit, and half-truths.

Filtering my thoughts for truth and error is a constant exercise for me. I find it easy to lie to myself. I can preach what I consider to be a poor sermon and berate myself with thoughts like *I am the worst preacher who ever preached.*

Is that true? No. The truth is, maybe last Sunday was not my best, but, thankfully, I have another chance next week.

I can come home after a demoralizing elders meeting and feel isolated and alone. *Nobody loves me,* I think. Is this true? No. This is not God speaking. I am speaking lies to myself. Julie loves me. My mother loves me. God loves me. There are a lot of people who love me. I can forget an important surgery and know I lost points with an influential family. Soon I am telling myself, *I can't do anything right.* Is this true? No. I do lots of things right.

I want no lies or half-truths in my mind. Life is hard enough to handle with the truth; it is impossible to navigate successfully when the mind is filled with lies and deceit.

9. *God's voice always leads to a deep, abiding sense of peace.* I believe that "the peace of God, which transcends all understanding, will guard your hearts and your minds in Christ Jesus" (Phil. 4:7). When God speaks I have a deep sense of peace.

When I played basketball, the referee's whistle stopped everything. I consider the peace of God to be like a referee with his whistle. When I am not hearing God clearly, the Holy Spirit blows his whistle to stop the game with a lack of peace and stirring unrest in my inner being. On the other hand, when I am playing well, the game proceeds smoothly and I have a deep sense of peace.

The spiritual adviser test

Of course, the above guidelines are just that—guidelines. I never act solely on the basis of what I hear in my inner spirit. I seek counsel from trusted advisers who help me verify if I am on the right track. "Many advisers make victory sure" (Prov. 11:14), wrote Solomon with good common sense. "A matter must be established by the testimony of two or three witnesses" (Deut. 19:15; Matt. 18:16) taught both Moses and Jesus, with good reason. These verses remind me never to strike out in word or in action without first testing what I think God has said with trusted spiritual advisers.

Several years after coming to Tucson, the stress and responsibility of a growing church precipitated in me a major crisis of confidence. I wondered if perhaps it was time to leave the ministry and find a new career. Weeks of prayer and seeking God left me confused; I concluded that my career in full-time ministry was over. I took my family to my parents' home in Dallas, where I grew up, to rest and sort through the issues before making a final decision. My dad and I went golfing one afternoon and were walking down the fourteenth fairway when I got the courage to mention my struggles. He was retired and spent many days playing golf for fun and enjoyment. He said nothing until we neared our drives in the middle of the fairway. Then he turned to me and said, "Whenever I reach a point where my golf game is struggling, I don't go buy a tennis racket and take up tennis. I get a golf lesson from the pro and work to become a better golfer."

I knew in an instant God had spoken. I would not sell insurance. I would seek advice and hone my skills and develop the expertise needed to pastor—and survive.

It used to bother me when one of my ideas was shot down in a meeting with church leaders—especially when I felt God had spoken. But now the words "Roger, you really don't want to do that" are no longer a threat. Instead, I often see them as the reasoned voice of wise counselors who help me understand what God is—and isn't—saying.

I want to hear God speak. I want to recognize God's voice and not be deceived by Satan's voice or my own. Undoubtedly, I will make mistakes in recognizing God's voice. However, the only thing worse than making mistakes is not listening for him in the first place. Now whenever someone calls or corners me at the door after church, and announces that they have a word from the Lord for the church or for me, I ask them how they know the message came from God. I find my checklist most helpful in carefully evaluating their response!

4

WATERING THE GARDEN

HE ROLLED DOWN THE WINDOW as he sped with his family down the street in front of our church. He raised his hand to his face, thumb to nose, and waved four fingers back and forth in front of his eyes as he launched in our direction a universal gesture of disgust and disrespect.

Shortly thereafter I listened intently as his daughter described his action to me. It would not have bothered me quite so much had he not been one of our deacons. How could a spiritual leader act so immaturely? He was a deacon but he was not a spiritual leader.

I would like to say he was already on the deacon board when I came to pastor the church. But he was not. He was one of the first new wave of deacons selected under my leadership. During the next year, our deacon body struggled. Votes were split six to eight or five to nine. One evening I got so frustrated I called for a halt: "I propose we cease all deacons' meetings while I do an intensive study on New Testament church organization and leadership. I will report back in six months."

I was surprised at the unanimous response to my proposal. No one else was having much fun either.

My study precipitated numerous changes in our church structure, but my most significant personal conclusion was that unspiritual people could never lead a church spiritually. Simply put, spiritual people hear God best. Our church was organized to select deacons and leaders. However, there was no machinery in place to ensure that the people selected were spiritually mature. I concluded that spiritual people became spiritual because they invested heavily in cultivating their inner human spirits.

It is easier to be smart and well-refined than it is to be spiritual. I know that spiritual maturity does not occur automatically. A well-functioning inner spirit must be cultivated. Paul prayed often for the inner spiritual development of his charges. For example, he told the Ephesians: "I pray that out of his glorious riches he may strengthen you with power through his Spirit in your inner being, so that Christ may dwell in your hearts through faith. And I pray that . . . you may be filled to the measure of all the fullness of God" (3:16–19).

During this time, I developed a model for cultivating my inner spirit. It's all too easy for pastors, as well as laypeople, to stay immature spiritually. Here is my model for being filled to the measure of all the fullness of God:

1. *Practice the disciplines.*I never knew spiritual disciplines formally existed until I read Richard Foster's book *The Celebration of Discipline.*[1] He details the activ-

---

[1] Richard Foster, *The Celebration of Discipline* (New York: Harper & Row, 1978).

ities that have brought spiritual growth and cultivation of the inner spirit to the faithful for two thousand years. I discovered I already practiced several
disciplines, such as prayer, service, worship, submission, confession, study, and celebration. Several others, however, were not part of my everyday Christian
experience: meditation, fasting, simplicity, solitude,
and guidance. I vowed to implement these into my
life.

For example, I decided to practice fasting. I learned
that fasting is abstaining from food for spiritual purposes. A normal fast involves abstaining from all
foods, but not from water (liquids). An absolute fast,
no food or water, is reserved for extreme circumstances and never lasts more than three days except by
supernatural empowerment. Of course, people with
medical problems need to check with their doctors
before beginning to fast.

I discovered the Bible reveals various reasons for
fasting: I fast when I want to know God's will—such
as whether to hire a new staff member or to relocate
the church (Acts 13:2). I fast before long, dangerous
journeys—mission trips to the Ukraine or Turkey
(Ezra 8:21–23). I fast to humble myself before God—
when I am overcome with pride, selfish ambition, or a
spirit of competition (Deuteronomy 8:2–14). I fast
when I want to get God's attention—such as when my
daughter was dying (Joel 2:12; 1 Kings 21:20–29; and
2 Samuel 12:22–23). I fast when I need to overcome a
stronghold in my life—such as overeating (Isaiah

58:6). I fast for protection and physical safety—such as before I had my colon removed (Esther 4:15–16). I fast to enhance my worship of God—on Saturdays before Sunday services (Luke 2:37).

I began with a one-meal fast and gradually increased to fasts of three days or longer. Normally I fast for either twenty-four hours or for three days, depending on what I sense to be the prompting of the Holy Spirit. I learned not to begin with a long fast. The body grows accustomed to fasting by degrees. Arthur Wallis's book *God's Chosen Fast* was a helpful resource in learning about this spiritual discipline.[2]

2. Listen deep in the inner spirit. Julie and I used to select a spiritual subject or biblical topic to study while on vacation. (Unfortunately, the practice died out when our children arrived.) We were inching along in a rental car through a construction zone outside of Pittsburgh, when Julie looked at me and said, "We haven't picked a subject for this vacation. What do you want to study?"

I had nothing in mind, so I was pleased when she continued.

"Have you ever heard a sermon on the human spirit?" she asked. "The Bible has a lot to say about body, soul, and spirit. Do you know the difference between a soul and a spirit?"

"No, I have never heard a sermon on that, and no,

---

[2]Arthur Wallis, *God's Chosen Fast* (Fort Washington, Pa.: Christian Literature Crusade, 1977).

I don't know the difference between a soul and a spirit."

We had our vacation study subject. We were intrigued by Paul's statement in 1 Corinthians 14:15, "I will pray with my spirit . . . [and] with my mind; I will sing with my spirit . . . [and] with my mind." And in 1 Corinthians 2:10–13, Paul describes how the Holy Spirit expresses spiritual words to our inner, human spirit. Our summer study led toward a deeper intimacy with God as we began to cultivate the art of listening for God to communicate with us—Holy Spirit to human spirit. We discovered the human spirit is our organ for God-consciousness and the seat of our communion with God, where he longs to minister to and fellowship with us.

Listening for the voice of God in my inner spirit was not easy at first. I had to learn to quiet my mind if I were to hear the "still, small voice." My mind was active and undisciplined. There were too many things I wanted to think about.

The human brain operates at different speeds. In deep sleep, the brain slows to zero to three cycles per second (the delta wave). The brain moves toward increasing levels of wakefulness at four to seven cycles per second (the theta wave). The alpha wave, eight to thirteen cycles per second, is best for creativity and contemplation—such as for communing with God and hearing God speak. Most Americans, however, spend the bulk of their waking hours in the more rapid beta-wave level of brain activity. This speed, fourteen to twenty-five cycles per second, is perfectly suited for baking casseroles, going to meetings, and solving problems. Unfortunately, it is possible to live at even faster levels of brain intensity. As the cycles increase, we find ourselves in hassled, hurried, frenzied states of mind. I am convinced much of my struggle in learning to hear God speak resulted from a fast-paced life in a rapid-fire, imagery-oriented society, which tended to overload my mental circuits and distract me from hearing the voice of God, just as surely as massive radio jamming kept the Gospel out of many Communist countries during the cold war.

The first time I tried to slow down my mind and sit quietly before God, I found my thoughts wandered everywhere. Hearing God's still, small voice was well nigh impossible when thinking about tomorrow's lunch appointment, or next Sunday's sermon, or the balance in my checkbook, or Deacon Smith's surgery that I forgot. I could travel from my driveway to the rings of Saturn in seconds. I had to acquire new skills to focus my listening habits. So I practiced taking my runaway thoughts "captive" as Paul encourages in 2 Corinthians 10:5. Two things helped as I learned to meditate.

First, I set aside time to quiet down and make a conscious choice to calm my soul. When I was in college, Julie challenged me to memorize Psalm 131 in the *Revised Standard Version*. It is one of the Songs of Ascents that lead to the worship of God. David wrote:

O Lord, my heart is not lifted up,
   my eyes are not raised too high;
I do not occupy myself with things
   too great and too marvelous for me.
But I have calmed and quieted my soul,
   like a child quieted at its mother's
      breast;
   like a child that is quieted is my soul.

I noted that David had a choice. And so did I. He could let his mind run away if he wanted to, or he could quiet his mind and not worry about all the big issues that bombarded his life. So could I.

Second, I utilized Madame Guyon's guidelines for quieting the mind in *Experiencing the Depths of Jesus Christ*.[3] She recommended focusing on a Bible passage (such as Psalm 23) or meditating on a comforting image of Christ (such as the Lord ministering to the woman caught in the act of adultery in John 8). At first I was able to sit quietly only for minutes at a time. Soon minutes turned into quarter-hours, then half-hours, and occasionally hours. I learned to concentrate and pray slowly through the Scriptures or meditate on Christ until my mind was sufficiently settled. Then I listened for God's Spirit to speak deep within.

I believe this is a small part of what Paul meant when he discussed "praying in his spirit." I pray with

---

[3]Madame Guyon, *Experiencing the Depths of Jesus Christ* (Goleta, Calif.: Christian Books, 1975).

my mind by working through a prayer list and by consciously praying for the things I know need prayer. Then, when the list is complete, I quiet my mind and seek to commune with God in my spirit. I listen for God's voice and sense his promptings to pray for people and for situations that would normally never come to my mind. My most precious experiences occur when God speaks by his Holy Spirit to my human spirit.

Once I began to control my mind, I found I no longer needed to find a special place or dedicate a formal time to commune with God. I could do it anytime, anywhere. A heated church business meeting put my ability to hear God anywhere to the test. The fight centered on whether to buy inexpensive wooden baby cribs or to purchase the more expensive, easier-to-clean, and longer-lasting metal ones. My anxiety increased as the arguing continued and the tension rose.

If I could find inner peace with God in that mess, I could enjoy God anywhere. I mentally disengaged from the heated discussion and sought the Spirit of God deep within. The peace was comforting as the storm swirled and God and I communed Holy Spirit to human spirit.

3. Obey God's promptings. When I sense God speaking, I am careful to obey him. Each time I do, I believe my spirit is strengthened and matured, and I am better equipped to hear again. On the other hand, if I refuse to obey, my spirit shrivels and darkens, and it becomes harder to hear.

Responding favorably to God begins with following my conscience. When I was a boy, I heard many sermons on the sinfulness of smoking, drinking, and dancing. Were these teachings biblical? Not necessarily. But they were acceptable Baptist theology in the days of my youth. Being a good Baptist, I never smoked, drank, or learned to dance.

In my ninth grade year, I was nominated for homecoming king in junior high school. The winner was to be announced at an all-school dance where the new king and queen danced the first dance of the evening.

I struggled with my conscience all week: Should I go to the dance? I was taught that a good Baptist, especially one called to preach, would not even attend a dance. Surely it could not be so bad just to go. But what if I won? Should I take the queen in my arms and try to dance the first dance—or politely decline and stammer out some explanation about how good Christians don't dance? What I needed was a good case of the flu or the throw-up virus or a broken leg or something to give me a good excuse not to attend. But Saturday came and I was healthy and intact, so I stifled my screaming conscience, put on my best suit, and went to the dance. I may have been the only homecoming nominee in America that year who pleaded with God to lose. I was horrified when my name was announced as king. The music began and the new queen and I were ushered onto the dance floor. Everything happened so fast. The teachers were smiling, and the students were clapping.

But I could not dance—partly because I was not sure how, and mostly because my raging conscience told me I was on the verge of committing a sin and ruining my testimony for Jesus Christ. I stammered out some half-whispered statement that good Baptists don't dance and walked off the floor. One of the teachers asked another nominee to dance in my place, and the party went on.

A conscience is a delicate thing. One of God's internal tools, a conscience is implanted by God to give general direction concerning right and wrong. But the values, moral truths, and rules a society shares and agrees to live by also shape many of the specifics in the conscience. From a biblical point of view, a *strong* conscience is trained to align closely with biblical truth. A *weak* conscience is one filled with all sorts of traditions, ideas, and customs taught to be biblical but that have little to do with the revealed Word of God.

The pastor, church leaders, and teachers at whose feet I sat for my most formative years, infused into my life and conscience many powerful biblical concepts. Nevertheless, as happens in all church settings, they also built into my life some church traditions and expectations that weakened—instead of strengthened—my conscience. The Bible condemns the misuse of alcohol, not its consumption. (Of course, it needs to be pointed out, especially in our society, that the misuse of alcohol has brought devastation to many.) Smoking is not mentioned in the Bible. Dancing is portrayed in the Scriptures as a normal activity useful in both worship and human socialization. My conscience was trained to believe these were all sins. In these areas, my conscience was weak.

In Romans 14, Paul discussed the issue of meat offered to idols. Christians with strong consciences realized no sin was involved, so Paul encouraged them to eat the meat. On the other hand, those with weak consciences believed that eating the meat was sinful, so Paul counseled them to follow their consciences and not eat. God expected them to follow the inner promptings of their consciences even if they were poorly trained—so critical is a positive response to the promptings deep within. Of course, God did not intend for them to live all of their lives with weak consciences. He intended for them to retrain and strengthen their consciences in areas where they were weak.

While I am now convinced there is nothing wrong with dancing—my conscience is retrained and more closely aligned with biblical truth—I was right not to dance that night. I would have sinned by sweeping the queen off her feet, violating my conscience. Paul's comment in Romans 14:23, "The man who has doubts is condemned if he eats," explains how the same activity can be a sin for one person and not for another. My wife grew up in a Baptist church across town from me. Her pastor never made dancing a test of biblical

Christianity, and thus she danced her way through school without sinning (and probably had a lot more fun than I did!).

In cultivating my inner spirit, I try always to follow the promptings of my conscience. Of course, the conscience is only one small part of the inner workings of my spirit. Therefore, whenever I sense God speaking anywhere in my inner being, I intend to respond favorably. I mature my spirit and thus improve my ability to hear him speak by doing what God leads me to do. I hurt my spirit when I disobey or refuse.

One-sentence sermon

About thirty minutes into our weekly Saturday night prayer meeting, I heard a quiet voice inside say, *Roger, instead of preaching your sermon in the morning, I want you to walk to the pulpit and say, "It is not possible to be content with your sins and really be a Christian." Then turn and walk off the platform.*

I paused. *That was a funny thought.* Then I went back to praying. About ten minutes later, the voice returned. *Roger, in the morning, I want you to walk to the pulpit and say, "It is not possible to be content with your sins and really be a Christian." Then turn and walk off the platform.* The second time got my attention, and I began struggling: Was that God speaking to me? Or did I just make this up? Or was it some sort of satanic temptation to do something stupid?

Later, when the prayer meeting was over and everyone had left our house, I sat down with Julie and told her, "I just had the strangest thing happen to me."

Julie listened carefully, and when I finished, her first words were "You're not really going to do that, are you?"

"I don't know. My sermon's ready. It's not like I'm unprepared. If I get up and say just one sentence, the people are going to think I'm nuts."

"You'd better be careful. You could lose your job over something like this."

"I know."

The next morning Julie's first words were "You're not really going to do that, are you?"

After spending time in prayer, I felt convinced God was speaking. However, I love to preach; I could not think of many things more humiliating than to stand behind a pulpit and, before God and the people, do a strange thing.

Early that morning I gathered with our ministers for prayer. As I prepared to tell them what I intended to do, God said, *No. You may not tell them anything about this.*

The first service commenced. The hymns were sung, the offering was taken, the special music was completed, and it was my turn to preach. I walked to the pulpit, took a deep breath, and spoke right into the microphone: "It is not possible to be content with your sins and really be a Christian." Then I turned and walked off the platform. As I passed the worship leader, he whispered, "Where are you going? Where are you going?"

I had no freedom to tell. This was between God and me, alone.

I walked down the steps, out the door, around the side of the church, back to my office; opened the door, went inside, locked the door, got down on my knees and wept: "God, how could you do this to me? God, this is so humiliating. I can't believe you made me do this. They are going to think I'm nuts. I'm going to get fired."

Things were not much better back in the worship service. Pandemonium was breaking out. People were asking, "Did he just resign?"

Some said, "No, I think he had a nervous breakdown."

We had three morning services then, so I returned to preach my one-sentence sermon a second time and then a third. I would like to say that lives were changed, that hundreds decided to follow Christ. The truth is, hardly anyone ever mentioned it. I received only one letter commenting on it. Finally, it began to dawn on me that my one-sentence sermon was not for the congregation. That sermon was for me: Did I really want to hear God speak, even if obedience produced one of the most humiliating experiences of my life?

My innermost spirit matured a lot that day. Hearing God speak can carry a high price tag, though usually not. I cultivate my inner spirit because I love to commune with God. I enjoy sharing intimate thoughts and feelings with him. I practice the spiritual disciplines. I try to obey my conscience and keep it strong. While I make some mistakes in discerning what God says, I enjoy getting to know God, and I want to become a spiritual man with a strong spirit.

5

OVERCOMING THE EVIL ONE

I HAD NO PREVIOUS EXPERIENCE with demons or spiritual forces the day my future wife and I went to visit Harry in a small rural hospital near the church where I pastored part time during college. He had suffered a serious heart attack and been in a coma ever since. We arrived near lunchtime, and encouraged his wife to take a much-needed break while we stayed with her husband.

After talking to Harry, Julie and I decided to pray for him. Shortly after we began, he moved his lips and said, "Jesus Christ did not come in the flesh."

Stunned, Julie and I immediately thought of 1 John 4:2: "Every spirit that acknowledges that Jesus Christ has come in the flesh is from God, but every spirit that does not acknowledge Jesus is not from God. This is the spirit of the antichrist." Julie began to cry. I wanted to.

Perhaps by divine design, we had studied about the Gadarene demoniac in a "Life and Teachings of Christ" course just that morning at Baylor University. The professor said, "Jesus always found out the demon's name before casting it out."

I said to Julie, "Let's pray, and ask for a name." We bowed our heads and demanded in the name of Christ that if we were dealing with a demonic spirit, it must reveal its name.

Much to our surprise, Harry spoke: "My name is Clarissus."

We were speechless and terrified. After calming down, Julie asked, "What do we do now?"

"I don't know," I replied. "The dismissal bell rang this morning and that's as far as we got" (which was the truth).

"Then why don't we do what Jesus did?" Julie suggested. "Let's pray for Clarissus to come out."

So we bowed our heads and prayed for Clarissus to come forth. Nothing happened.

Shortly afterward, Harry's wife returned. "How did things go?" she asked.

Julie looked at me, and I looked at her. We weren't about to tell her what happened. The truth is, we were not certain ourselves.

"Just fine," we said.

We were in the parking lot when Harry's wife came running out the hospital door yelling, "Wait! Wait! What happened in there? Something's happened to Harry! I want to know what happened."

Frightened, we said not a word.

About 10:30 that evening, Harry regained consciousness and said to his wife, "I just had the strangest dream. I was climbing the steps to heaven and St. Peter said, 'You can't come in now.' So I climbed back down the ladder. I guess God has more things for me to do before I die."

Ten minutes later he had a massive heart attack. Three days later I conducted his funeral.

Then I had a hundred questions about what happened that day, and Harry wasn't around to answer them. But in the twenty-five years since that intriguing Thursday afternoon in central Texas, I have invested considerable energy in thinking about how spiritual forces oppress pastors in two areas: in our personal lives, and in how we care for people who have opened their lives to the Evil One and suffered spiritual attack. Overcoming the devil is a must-learn skill in the process of spiritual growth (1 John 2:12–14).

Spiritual warfare in our personal life

If I were the devil, I'd wage warfare against pastors. I'd attack relentlessly with spirits of depression and despair, anger and bitterness, jealousy and lust, deceit and pride. I'd motivate all sorts of people and hosts of demonic forces to make pastoral life miserable. In addition, I would make sure all pastors memorized early in their careers the passage, "Greater is he that is in you than he that is in the world" (1 John 4:4, KJV). Then, I would wreak havoc while pastors assumed divine immunity from my attacks. I would hide while they sought help everywhere but the one place where they might find relief.

One of the most vicious satanic attacks I've withstood began one Sunday during the closing moments of the evening service. An impression of impending death overwhelmed me. I felt I had just preached my last sermon. I would die before next Sunday. I sat in dread in the blue rocking chair in our living room late into the next two nights, waiting to die. Strange tinglings moved down my arms. Tuesday morning I called a cardiologist friend at University Hospital, and within hours I was on a treadmill undergoing all sorts of heart tests. When all checked out well, the cardiologist called the chief of neurology, and thirty minutes later I was in his office undergoing a neurological exam.

"Your symptoms don't fit any of the usual neurological problems or diseases," he said. "Perhaps you have some exotic problem I have never encountered. Other than that, I don't know what to tell you. I advise you to go on home, resume your normal activity, and see if any other symptoms develop."

But the oppression did not abate. Late Thursday afternoon I was exercising on my NordicTrack when a counselor from one of our deliverance teams called. "I really hate to bother you," he began, "but we had something happen that may interest you. A woman struggling to get out of witchcraft just revealed in a deliverance session that she and some of her friends had placed a curse on you. They actually prayed for a spirit of death to destroy you. I know this is probably nothing, and I almost didn't call, but perhaps you'll find the information useful."

I got back on the exercise machine and shouted out praise and thanksgiving to God. Then I rebuked the spirits attacking me, and immediately the oppression lifted. The symptoms dissipated.

Most spiritual attacks are not nearly so dramatic. I would be hard pressed to tell another story like that one. However, over extended periods, less intensive attacks can be just as devastating. Subtle attacks often go undiagnosed for years. Many pastors rarely consider that their depression, despair, envy, anger, bitterness, jealousy, lust, deceit, or pride may have a spiritual-warfare component.

Worry was one of my besetting sins. I can spiritualize it and call it "unbelief" or a "lack of faith," because those words sound better, but they fail to disguise the ugliness of my problem. Living in the future and brooding about the past siphoned off needed energy from my wife, children, and church family.

My day off was the worst. My wife often told me how much she hated Fridays. Without pressing church problems to distract me, I was free to brood about all sorts of problems.

"You're acting like a preoccupied, intimidated child," Julie said to me on many occasions. "Now stop it. You're no fun to be around."

Like most worriers, I had observed that at least 99 percent of what I worried about never happened, but I could not stop. I was miserable. One day, while navigating through a worrisome fog of "what ifs," I wondered if I had persisted in uncontrolled worry for so long that Satan had gained a foothold in my life (Ephesians 4:27). Perhaps I was not only fighting the flesh; I was fighting the devil as well.

The process I used to find relief from my worry I now use often when I suspect a spiritual attack. James 4:7 gives a simple formula: "Submit yourselves, then, to God. Resist the devil, and he will flee from you." For me, submitting to God involves three things: (1) confessing that the area is out of control and needs help; (2) consciously yielding the area to God; and (3) considering myself dead, according to Romans 6, to the sin in that area. If these three activities provide freedom, then I thank God the problem was only a sin of the flesh. However, if the struggle persists, I consider that I may be experiencing a spiritual attack. The second half of James 4:7—"Resist the devil"—then comes into play.

Resisting the devil addresses the spiritual forces attacking my life. Finding freedom involves four things: (1) declaring that I have forsaken and confessed my sin to God so the forces of evil no longer have a foothold; (2) renouncing the attacking forces ("In the name of Jesus Christ, depart and leave me alone. I rebuke you and your attacks against me. I want nothing to do with you."); (3) asking for the filling of the Holy Spirit; and (4) imploring the Holy Spirit to build a hedge of protection around me from future attacks. (If God can build a hedge around Job—Job 1:10—then he can build one around me. Also, I often ask God not to lower my hedge like he lowered Job's. I figure it can't hurt to ask!)

I believe it is easier to avoid a spiritual attack than

to struggle through one later. Just as I never leave the house in the morning without my clothes, I never leave without my spiritual armor. Every day I specifically pray for the spiritual armor of Ephesians 6:10–17. I also pray daily for God to erect that spiritual hedge around my family, my church, and me.

Spiritual warfare is always a prayer project. Prayer provides protection prior to attack. Prayer provides offensive weapons to neutralize attacking spiritual forces. Prayer provides healing balm for recovery from inflicted spiritual wounds.

Spiritual warfare in our work

The man from the utility company finished his work and said, "You're Roger Barrier, aren't you? I listen to your radio program every day. My wife and I are both Christians. She's having some problems; in fact, there are times when I wonder what's going on inside of her. Do you believe in demons?"

"Yes," I replied. "Why don't we sit down in the kitchen and talk?"

"Several months ago," he began, "we went to a spiritualist church where we were encouraged to pray to receive spirit guides to help direct our lives. I didn't pray for any, but my wife did. She hasn't been the same since. Sometimes, it's as if there's a different person inside. Her voice changes; her face contorts; she has an aversion to the things of God. Our marriage is falling apart. She won't go back to our Christian

91

church. It all came to a head last night. While we were arguing, she walked into the hallway, turned slowly, and said with a sneer, 'Don't you know who we are?' Her voice rose to a scream as she repeated, 'Don't you know who we are? Don't you know who we are?'"

He was shaking now.

"I think," he said, "she is demon-possessed, like they talk about in the Bible. Can you help us?"

My affirmative answer was easy to say. But reaching the point where I felt confident to say it was not.

Today Casas Adobes sponsors a deliverance ministry, which developed because of people who sought help for problems that could only be described as demonic. As we began caring for these folks, some in our congregation were upset. Some were convinced that demons existed only in the first-century world. Others were indignant; most were ignorant of spiritual-warfare issues.

A key turning point was when our counseling pastor grew frustrated working with people who should have found emotional healing for their personal problems, reconciliation for their marriages, and harmony in their relationships—but never did. Well-trained by every secular standard in both counseling and psychology, our counseling pastor lamented that the success rate in the psychiatric field hovered around 10 percent.

When he added the spiritual-warfare component to his tools for helping people, he discovered that people who were not helped in any other way began finding victory. When a problem does not yield to medical attention, standard psychological counseling, biblical insight, or the usual prayer requests, it is not unwise to consider the possibility of a spiritual attack.

Deliverance checklist

Alan came to my office late one afternoon after everyone had left for the day. Over the years his childhood devotion to Christ had waned. Unfortunately, he responded to his spiritual longings by attending a spiritualist church. When the leaders asked if he wanted a spirit guide to help him through life, he responded enthusiastically.

Now he was no longer enthusiastic.

He told me, "I received something that night, and I don't like what I got." I looked on with amazement as he went into a trance. His eyes had a glazed, faraway look. After a while he came back to himself and said simply, "They're back, aren't they."

I was not quite certain who "they" were, but I agreed—they seemed to be back.

I excused myself and called another of our pastors, who was at home, to return to the office. I did not want to be alone with Alan. When the other pastor arrived, Alan detailed the symptoms of his problem, which ranged from astral projection to demonic visions. I never cease to be amazed at unsuspecting Christians who use a demonic tool to open the door to the occult. Our deliverance ministry has a checklist of past activities for people to examine:

- Contact with occult activity (Deuteronomy 18:9–13)
- Personal invitation for demonic guidance and help (2 Corinthians 11:4)
- Drug and alcohol abuse involvement (Ephesians 4:20–22)
- Perpetual sin (Ephesians 4:27)
- Transference (Exodus 20:5–6)
- An undisciplined or "out of control" mind (2 Corinthians 10:3–5)
- Sexual sin or abuse (Many deliverance sessions reveal that struggles in this area allow Satan to gain a foothold in a person's life.)

The above list is not exhaustive, but it is a good place to begin. Neil Anderson's *Seven Steps to Freedom*[1] is now our basic tool for helping people identify areas where they might have opened the door to occult activity. We encourage Christians to remove every occult influence by confession, repentance, and renunciation. Many people I shepherd have innocently entered into occultic activity—from palm readings at the fair to role-playing games at parties to fortune-tellers with crystal balls—with unfortunate long-term results.

Before he died, Dr. Walter Martin—a specialist on cults and occultic activity—and I were discussing

---

[1]Neil Anderson, *Seven Steps to Freedom* (Ventura, Calif.: Regal Books, n.d.).

satanic attacks against Christians. He said, "It is not paranoid for Christians to think that Satan is out to get them. I teach people that the areas of their lives that are not under the control of the Holy Spirit are open to control by demonic spirits."

Shortly after our chat, I used a concordance to underline every verse in the Bible that described Satan and his devices. My Bible oozed yellow highlighter. This exercise convinced me to prepare my congregation to protect themselves.

Let me summarize some areas in which we instruct our congregation in spiritual warfare:

- First-century Christians had trouble recognizing satanic attacks, and Christians still have trouble today. (2 Corinthians 2:11)
- Evangelism improves when we realize that many refuse Christ not because they love their sin, but because Satan blinds their eyes so that they cannot see the Gospel. (2 Corinthians 4:3–4)
- Satan's major tool is deception. Job was deceived (Job 3:25–26). Since perfect Eve was deceived (2 Corinthians 11:3), we who are imperfect must be doubly vulnerable to misdiagnosing Satan's intentions. (The word *occult* means "hidden.")
- The Bible constantly warns Christians to beware of satanic harm (Acts 13:10; 2 Corinthians 11:13–15; 2 Thessalonians 2:9–12; 1 Timothy 4:1; and 2 Timothy 3:13). His tools include lying (John 8:32, 44), anger (Ephesians 4:26–27), an unforgiving spirit (2

Corinthians 2:10–11), sin (Ephesians 2:12; 1 John 3:8–10), accusations and insinuations (Revelation 12:10), temptation (1 Corinthians 7:5; 1 Thessalonians 3:5), contact with the occult (Deuteronomy 18:10–13), and drug and alcohol abuse (Galatians 5:21).

While we provide instruction about spiritual warfare, we also point the way toward freedom in Christ. I read *The Adversary*,[2] a primer on spiritual warfare by Mark Bubeck, shortly before I counseled Alan about his spirit guides and astral projection. "I believe the biblical tools you need for victory," I said to Alan, "are outlined in this book. Read it, do what it says, and you will find freedom. If not, let me know and we'll take the next step."

I was running an experiment with Alan. Most of my deliverance experiences to that point involved direct encounters with the spirit world. I wanted to see if Alan could gain victory on his own with a more discipleship-oriented approach. He took the book, followed the biblical guidelines, prayed the suggested prayers, and found freedom. He has served faithfully in our church ever since. My experience is that people who struggle with demonic problems seldom need direct intervention. A Bible and some discipleship instruction provide all the help they need.

[2]Mark Bubeck, *The Adversary* (Chicago, Ill.: Moody Press, 1996).

Deliverance perspective

The only organized opposition I ever had against me in the past twenty-five years of pastoring came from individuals who were dead set against our ministry to those harassed by the occult. The pain of that experience still lingers. I have learned to be patient in developing a spiritual-warfare ministry within an established church. It needs to be done—but carefully and wisely.

Since the work of a deliverance ministry involves the occult, those who minister in such a work need to be maturing Christians—not spiritual children. Spiritual young men—not children—are the ones who have overcome the Evil One (1 John 2:12–14).

A word of caution: I watched a pastor lose his church because he became so involved in deliverance work, he had little time or energy left for his other pastoral duties. As I made myself available for deliverance work, I discovered that Satan was delighted to bring me into contact with demonically attacked people from all over town. Not only was the experience oppressive, it was time intensive. While I helped pioneer the spiritual-warfare ministry, I soon after turned it over to others. It gets no more time from me than other church ministries.

Few events demonstrate the power of God more than watching the Spirit of God overcome the forces of evil. I worked for several hours with a woman who was spiritually overwhelmed. She hardly moved or changed facial expression as I demanded in the name of Christ that the numerous spirits who kept talking through her be silenced. I wanted to speak directly with her. No one in the room that day will forget her face—frozen, locked in stone, a tear trickling out of the corner of her left eye—the moment I asked her if she wanted to receive Christ. Her lips moved, and an almost imperceptible "yes" came out of her mouth. Soon she was free.

I remember the night a woman raced toward me screaming, "I am going to gouge your eyes out." A raised hand and a command in Jesus' name brought her to her knees. For the first time, I felt I understood what the seventy-two disciples meant in Luke 10:17 when they returned from their mission, awed with Jesus' power over demons, and said excitedly, "Lord, even the demons submit to us in your name." Christ immediately put deliverance work in perspective: "Do not rejoice that the spirits submit to you, but rejoice that your names are written in heaven" (Luke 10:20).

Greater is he that is in you than he that is in the world.

6

GUIDANCE FOR SUFFERING

PAIN ETCHED SALLY'S FACE. Nerves damaged by radiation treatments left her in constant agony. "The doctors say they can do nothing more," she said. "God is my only hope. I noticed a passage on healing in James 5 yesterday that might help."

As she opened her Bible, I saw two verses underlined in red: "Is any one of you sick? He should call the elders of the church to pray over him and anoint him with oil in the name of the Lord. And the prayer offered in faith will make the sick person well; the Lord will raise him up."

"Would you please gather the elders and pray for me?" she asked.

It wasn't that simple.

I grew up in a denomination that ill-prepared me for her request. The unwritten but strongly implied rule of our denominational culture stated that pastors who ministered in the area of healing were charismatic at best and deluded at worst. Also, our churches were organized around deacons; we had no elders. Furthermore, I was not sure what a "prayer of faith" was. Finally, I had never anointed anyone with oil and was not certain how to do it.

I chose my words carefully: "Sally, you are the first

person to ask me to pray for healing according to James 5. I am not certain what to do." I explained my pastoral dilemma and then proposed a solution: "I suggest that we both pray and fast for five days. I'll meet you in my office next Friday afternoon, and if God tells us to proceed, we will."

Sally was no novice. She had walked with God for many years. She agreed to the proposal.

Five days later we both wrote on paper what we thought God told us and then exchanged papers. The conclusions were identical. We made plans for a healing service on Sunday afternoon. Since we had no elders at the time, I invited our deacons.

During the thirty minutes before Sally arrived, I explained to the deacons her request, the background to her pain, and what I knew of James 5:14–15. I asked if anyone had participated in a healing service before. No hands raised.

When Sally arrived, we asked her to confess any known sin, because James mentions this in verse 16. When she finished, I took the bottle from Lucky's Supermarket and prepared to pour olive oil over her head. One of the deacons averted a mess when he shook his head and whispered that a drop on a finger applied lightly to her forehead might work better. We took turns passing the bottle, anointing her with oil, and praying for her.

I wondered if perhaps Sally would now leap up like on television and shout, "Glory to God! I'm healed!" But nothing happened. As she quietly departed, she thanked us for our prayers and left a room filled with disappointed confusion mixed with a measure of hope.

Unknown to us, the healing service had just moved to another time and place. In the early morning hours, Sally was awakened by a strange sensation and knew instantly that she was healed. By the time she was out of bed, the pain was gone, never to return. Later Sally related to me an intriguing aside: "I think the reason God did not heal me in front of the deacons was because they might get proud. I think God waited until I was alone so he would get all the glory."

From that inauspicious beginning, God began to weave a physical healing ministry into our church fabric. I have developed a working theology of healing that is fashioned out of biblical texts, a solid dose of practical reality, and hours spent asking God for help in all sorts of complex situations.

Stepping out

Healing prayers are risky. When it appears that my prayers are not working, I feel embarrassed, like a failure. At times I have prayed for things that were flat-out wrong. Occasionally I have sensed pressure to pray for things that were not from God. Some prayers have produced the results I wanted, and some have not. Some people have gotten well, and some have died.

One time I prayed something that I knew in my inner spirit would not happen, but I prayed anyway because I wanted to give hope and encouragement to a young mother. Along with nine others, I was praying for a woman whose breast cancer had raged out of control. When the cancer was discovered early in her pregnancy, the doctors recommended an immediate abortion because chemotherapy would kill the unborn baby. At great risk to herself, she delayed the treatments and carried her child to term. The delay proved costly.

She lay dying as we gathered to pray the prayers of James 5. As I dipped my finger in the oil and placed it gently on her forehead, I knew deep in my spirit that she was going to die. Nevertheless, I prayed earnestly for God's healing and thanked him in advance that all would be well. I had lied in my prayer. Several months later I stood in deep snow in a lonely country cemetery in northern Arizona with her widowed husband and three children as they lowered her casket into the grave.

While that was not the first—or last—mistake I have made praying healing prayers, I've determined that the risk of a few embarrassing incidents is small compared to the joy and success that comes as a result of such prayers. I believe many people who would have remained sick were healed because our leaders followed the instructions of James 5.

Robert was a Wycliffe Bible translator who went into anaphylactic shock after being bitten by a desert insect. He was comatose by the time the emergency helicopter flew him to the hospital. His wife knew the odds for a full recovery were dim. The EEG showed not much was working. But her strong faith in God strengthened and inspired the many friends who had gathered in the lobby to pray.

As we circled and held hands, I told God there was no reason for Robert to die. He was young. He had children to raise. His New Testament translation was three-fourths done, and there was no need to let years of work go to waste. I told God that we desired a full recovery with no brain damage or long-term complications. I also told God we would yield to whatever he had in mind. Then I asked Christ to strengthen the family for any upcoming situation. I never mentioned James 5.

But a week later, his wife did.

"Would you gather the elders and come to the hospital and pray for my husband?" she asked.

After securing permission from the ICU nurse, eight men and I circled the bed of the unconscious Wycliffe translator. Before entering the ICU, we had prayed together and sensed a deep assurance that Robert would be healed. It was easy now to pray the prayer of faith and thank God for Robert's healing. While we prayed, I noticed several nurses and doctors peek in on the proceedings. Two hours after we left, his wife called: Robert was sitting up in bed asking for something to eat.

Interactive understanding

While this may seem elementary, I must say this up front: It is not always God's will to heal. He sometimes has other things in mind. In John 9 Jesus healed a man born blind: "His disciples asked him, 'Rabbi, who sinned, this man or his parents, that he was born blind?'

"'Neither this man nor his parents sinned,' said Jesus, 'but this happened so that the work of God might be displayed in his life.'"

The apostle Paul accomplished some powerful healing and resurrection miracles; however, he did not do it every time. He could not help his sick friend Epaphroditus (Philippians 2:25–27). He left Trophimus sick in Miletus (2 Timothy 4:20). Instead of sending Timothy to the local faith healer, Paul told him to drink a little wine for his stomach troubles. When Paul was unable to find relief from his "thorn," God sent Dr. Luke as his companion.

My first child, Jessie, was born to die young; she entered this world with a birth defect. Several hours after her birth, I struggled with God: "Why us? Why do we get the baby who's going to die? We've dedicated our lives to serving you. Is this all the thanks we get?"

Eight months later Jessie died in my arms. My wife and I watched her breath fade slowly. Finally Julie said, "Roger, she's gone." I placed my cheek to her nostrils and felt nothing. In unison Julie and I said, "Hi, Jessie. We're your Mommy and Daddy. We love you with all our hearts." We knew she was more alive then than ever before.

Several months after the funeral, I pondered why

Julie, Jessie, and I suffered through that experience. In the early days of my ministry, I hammered out a theology to explain why God allows sickness, suffering, and tragedies. The following checklist does not attempt to answer all the issues of evil in the world, but it helps me make sense out of life.

- Was Jessie's a sickness unto death? Yes, sometimes it is time to die. God never guarantees anyone a set number of years. Some live to the ripe age of eighty-five. Others fulfill their life destiny by the age of two.
- Was Jessie's sickness the result of some sin? The sins of the fathers are visited even to the third and fourth generation. I could think of all kinds of sins I had committed. If God wanted to punish me with a dying daughter, he had plenty of justification.
- Was this affliction for God's glory? God received glory from healing the blind man in John 9, and sometimes God allows trials and experiences to conform his children into the image of Christ.

While pondering that last question, I experienced one of those overwhelming moments when the Holy Spirit etches an impression deeply upon the heart. The message in my inner spirit was precise: *Roger, Jessie's sickness was no accident; it was designed for my glory. Do you know how much you hurt to have a baby unable to grow up physically?*

"Yes, Lord, I know, it hurts."

Then God impressed upon me, *Now you know how much I hurt when a Christian refuses to grow up spiritually*.

My entire ministry refocused that day toward helping Christians grow to spiritual maturity. Eternity will reveal how much glory God received as a result of Jessie's eight-month life.

Prayers for healing are not exercised solely on the basis of our faith, our will, or our wishes. They must also include a process that attempts to discern the will of God. When God's will is not discernible, the sick need guidance to pray for acceptance of whatever God may have in mind.

Word-based prayer

The prayer of faith does not demand a leap into the unknown. It is not positive thinking. It does not mean "to believe something so strongly that we make it come true" or that God must do what we believe. The prayer of faith does not rest on feelings or desires. It is based on a word from God. In every case, the heroes of Hebrews 11 based their faith on a word they heard from God.

The prayer of faith can be prayed only after God reveals his intentions. By definition, it is not possible to pray in faith when there has been no word from God. However, on those occasions when God makes his will clearly known, I find it exciting to pray and watch God work.

My first attempt at praying a prayer of faith

occurred when a young mother was rushed to the hospital with a brain aneurysm. As I walked down the hospital corridor, I contemplated what words of comfort I should say to her and what I should pray to God. I paused outside her door to seek God's will. Several moments later, I had a deep impression that she was going to be fine. I asked God if he were trying to tell me something. In my innermost being, I sensed God say that Rhonda's sickness was not unto death. She would survive with no complications and live to raise her children. An intense mental struggle ensued: *Was God really speaking to me? Was I just making this up? What if I told her what I heard and she died; I would look like a fool.*

However, I could not ignore the fact that immediately after I asked God how to handle this situation, I got a response.

When I walked into the room, Rhonda was awake, alert, and afraid. "Surgery is scheduled for Monday," she said. "The doctors want the swelling to subside before they operate. There is no guarantee that the artery will hold until then." Fear filled her eyes.

With all the courage I had, I looked into her eyes and said, "Rhonda, God told me that your sickness is not unto death. Whether the doctors will operate on Monday, I don't know, but you are going to be fine. Be at peace. All is well."

Never had I said words as bold and direct as these. The fear of embarrassment and risk diminished as I began praying for her healing. I reminded God that she had young children to raise, and there was no reason I could see why she should not be allowed to raise them. My prayer of faith rested on hearing a word from God.

Rhonda's surgery on Monday was a complete success. More than twenty years have passed since we prayed together in that hospital room. Her daughters are grown and married. She is alive and well.

The truth is, I usually have no idea what God intends when I pray alone or with our elders (we have some now) for the sick. In those cases, I pray a standard prayer based on James 4:2 ("You do not have, because you do not ask God"). I always ask God for a full recovery with no problems or long-term complications. I want no one to miss God's blessing because we failed to ask: "Father, you told us we could ask, so we did." Then I pray for submission to God's will: "Now, since we do not know your will in this case, we submit to what you have in mind. Your will be done." Finally, I ask God to pour into this person the power of Christ and to strengthen the family for any situation.

I want to add that going to a doctor does not invalidate earnest faith. Occasionally I encounter Christians who are afraid that seeking medical help symbolizes a lack of faith. These people need instruction. Christians are divided about the meaning of the anointing oil in James 5. Some anoint with oil as a sacred symbol of the Holy Spirit. Others believe the oil represented good first-century medical attention.

James may have had both meanings in mind. Two extremes are to be avoided: one is to pray with faith and refuse medical attention. The other is to resort to medical help and never pray.

God taught me a hard lesson about this: After suffering with an intestinal disease for almost a decade, I decided during seminary to pray in faith for God's healing. As a young, idealistic student searching for the boundaries of practical Christianity, I reasoned that taking cortisone and sulfa drugs was a sign of unbelief. I told God I would stop taking my medicine and place my full faith in him for my healing. In less than a month, I was hospitalized, and shortly thereafter the surgeon removed my entire colon. My "faith" was sinful, misguided presumption: "Thou shalt not put the Lord your God to the test." I encourage people to pray hard and seek the best medical help they can find. Faith plus modern medicine will bring wholeness to many.

What God loves to do

My favorite, most unusual divine healing happened one Sunday evening after church. A medical student approached me in tears. Cancerous lesions had appeared on her cervix, and she was meeting with her doctor in the morning to plan a course of action. Judy stood with her husband and poured out to me her fears of pain, suffering, and possible death. As a medical student, she knew better than most the risks and complications involved. If she did live, she might never have children. She wanted prayer according to James 5.

I invited several spiritual men and women to a corner of our then-deserted church auditorium to pray for her healing. When we finished, both she and her husband, Bill, thanked us and departed. The next morning Bill called.

"You'll never guess what happened after we got home," he said. "We were discussing the prayer time, and Judy said, 'I felt God's power on me tonight. Wasn't that exciting when the lighting crew turned that bright spotlight on me when Roger began to pray?'

"I said to her, 'What spotlight? Nobody turned on any bright light.'

"She said, 'Oh yes, there was a light. You mean you didn't see the light?'

"'No,' I replied. 'I did not see any bright light.' That's when we realized the tech crew had gone home much earlier. The bright light had to be from God."

The lesions were gone. She needed no surgery, no therapy, no treatment. She finished medical school, an internship, and residency; she and Bill now have two healthy children. God loves to heal, and he has much to say through the ministry of healing.

7

STEPS TOWARD HUMILITY

WHEN I STARTED OUT in pastoral work, I wanted to be the best pastor who ever lived. I wanted to do things for God that Moses never did. I wanted to accomplish such great things for the kingdom that the whole world would rise up and take note. I wanted to be the tool God used to bring revival to America. I wanted to build a big church, because I thought building a big church and being a successful pastor were the same thing. I imagined I would get to heaven and God would personally meet me at the gate and say something like, "You're finally here. We've been waiting for you. You're the best pastor we've ever had. Come and enjoy your Master's happiness!"

As I reflect on those lofty thoughts and note that each sentence begins with "I," I think of the words of Lucifer in Isaiah 14:13–14: "I will ascend to heaven; I will raise my throne above the stars of God; I will sit enthroned ... I will ... I will make myself like the Most High."

While I had no intention of becoming God, I was blind to my pride. I once heard that the only vitamin we all have too much of is Vitamin I. Pride is insidious. The more filled I am with pride, the more difficult it is to detect.

Several years into my first full-time pastorate, the number of Sunday services had multiplied. People sat in the foyer and on the sidewalks outside listening to my preaching from speakers. When people commended the success, I humbly told them that God was at work. He was. But so was I—and hard at it.

One day I read an article in *Christianity Today* on church growth by a man who had studied more than one hundred growing churches in America. He had interviewed more than fifty pastors and codified the common denominators that contributed to church growth, such as plenty of parking, vision for the future, creative programming, openness to new people, and an ability to raise money. The analyst then stuck a dagger into my heart when he concluded, "I have found among these pastors a deep passion to build a big church; however, I have not found a corresponding passion to know God."

I stared long and hard at the page. A wave of embarrassment and conviction overwhelmed me.

Was it possible that building a large church and being a good pastor were not the same? Was it possible to build a church and not have my soul knit tightly to God's? Was I mistaking my endeavors to bring glory to God and instead building a name for myself in disguise? Was I proud?

Yes, yes, yes, and yes.

A proud pastor is an ugly thing. Instead of displaying the glories of God, the proud pastor exalts fleshly ability. Instead of flowing with the message of God, the proud pastor is clogged with the pronouncements of self. Instead of experiencing the blessings of the Almighty, the proud pastor seeks satisfaction on the altar of human ability. Instead of emanating the sweet fragrance of the divine, the proud pastor stinks with an aroma of decay.

May God have mercy on my soul.

How do you apologize enough when you have used God's name and his church to build a name for yourself? How do you react when false humility is pulled back to reveal a heart dirtied with pride? I wept, confessed, and promised God I would sort out the issues and deal with my pride. I wanted to serve with humility in the vineyard he had entrusted to me.

One of the most devastating consequences of pride is the way it impairs our ability to hear God. In Psalm 138:6, David wrote, "Though the Lord is on high, he looks upon the lowly, but the proud he knows from afar." Some people are content with hearing God from afar. However, with the pressure of the ministry and considering the deep longings of my heart, I want close communion with, not estrangement from, God. In 2 Chronicles 7:14, God said, "If my people, who are called by my name, will humble themselves and pray and seek my face and turn from their wicked ways, then will I hear from heaven. . . ."

Humility must precede prayer. Before I can pray, I must deal with my pride. It is difficult to lead people when my pride stifles God's voice, through which he wants to lead me. I have assembled a list of questions that help me identify pride.

1. *Am I waking up at 3:00* A.M. *filled with anxiety?*The real issue is self-reliance. Whom do I trust to take care of the church, my family, and me? Pride is at work when I delude myself into thinking I am able to meet every need, to head off every problem.

One Christmas we drove 1,000 miles from Tucson to Dallas to spend the holidays with our folks. We were at a critical juncture in our church's history, and I was coming unglued. I hoped to find rest and solace in my parents' house where I grew up. Sleeping in my old bed and walking around the neighborhood often brought peace and restoration to my soul. But this time relief did not come. Night after night I awoke in terror, shaking with anxiety and fear, tormented with thoughts of impending doom.

Early one morning, unable to sleep, I got out of bed at three and walked into the den to think. Staring out the window into the darkened yard, I recalled the day I first crossed our backyard on my way to Walnut Hill School. Life was so simple then. Quietly I sensed God come near. *You are living as if I don't exist,* he whispered in my inner spirit. *Your lifestyle is the essence of pride. No wonder you are a wreck. Trust me. I can handle these problems. After all, I am God, and you're not.*

God reminded me of Isaiah 31:1: "Woe to those who go down to Egypt for help, who rely on horses, who trust in the multitude of their chariots and in the

118

great strength of their horsemen, but do not look to the Holy One of Israel." When anxiety, worry, or fear disturb my sleep too often, I know I am becoming my own Egypt.

2. Am I too busy to spend time with God?The workday begins, and my pride deludes me into thinking I have too much to do to spend time with God. Unless I get right to work, the church will fall apart. Soon I am trapped in frenzied activity that leaves me exhausted and stressed out.

My lifestyle was harried in the months before we traveled to Dallas. The morning after God spoke to me by the window, I opened my Bible and discovered a note I had written beside Isaiah 30:15–17, ten years earlier: "From Bill Nicholson to me during a time of stress and anxiety over job pressures and new church building (10–8–87)." I held my breath as I followed the arrow to the Scripture Bill intended for me to ponder: "In repentance and rest is your salvation, in quietness and trust is your strength, but you would have none of it. . . . A thousand will flee at the threat of one; at the threat of five you will all flee away, till you are left like a flagstaff on a mountaintop, like a banner on a hill."

Has nothing changed in ten years? I thought. *Bill could have pointed me here this week.*

It was December 23, 1997, and Isaiah described exactly how I felt—alone and abandoned—like a flagstaff on a mountaintop, like a lonely banner on a hill.

I vowed never again to live on my own without God. No matter how busy I think I have to be, nothing is more important than repentance, rest, quietness, and trust. To ignore these as unnecessary is a sign of pride.

3. Do I feel like I'm driving with the parking brake on? When pride creeps in, all of a sudden the work gets hard. Pastoring is no longer a delight. Instead, ministry becomes a heroic effort to rescue my plans and intentions. I believe this struggle is the outworking of James 4:6: "God opposes the proud but gives grace to the humble." Since God hates pride, he does whatever is necessary to deal with it. The apostle Paul's thorn was designed to thwart his pride: "To keep me from becoming conceited because of these surpassingly great revelations, there was given me a thorn in my flesh" (2 Cor. 12:7).

Not all problems are the result of God's opposition to pride. James taught that it was possible to distinguish between normal, everyday struggles and God's steadfast opposition to the swelling of self. In the context of trials, James wrote, "If any of you lacks wisdom, he should ask God, who gives generously to all without finding fault, and it will be given to him" (James 1:5).

When I feel like I'm driving with the parking brake on, I need to ask myself: *Are my ministry headaches simply routine struggles of everyday life? Or are they the result of God's steadfast opposition to my pride?*

The answers are critical. The first place to begin to

find them is to ask God for wisdom.

4. *Is people's approval sweet to my taste?* One morning I noticed an open spiral notebook on the bed. "Prayer List" was written across the top of the page in my wife's handwriting. I could not help myself; I picked it up and was humbled to discover the first seven requests were for me. Her first petition took my breath away: "Please deliver Roger from the fear of man, which will prove to be a snare" (Prov. 29:25).

I asked Julie, "What's this all about?"

"Remember when King Saul lost his kingdom?" she replied. "Samuel accused him of rebellion, arrogance, witchcraft, and disobedience. Remember Saul confessed that he had made a premature sacrifice because he was afraid of the people and so he gave in to them?

"I pray every day that you'll not fall into the trap of failing to do whatever God wants because you're afraid of what people might think."

I once heard Ralph and Lou Sutera, two revival leaders in Canada, identify the "pride of the praise of men" as "the temptation to bias intentions concerning actions and behavior according to what people think." They further described the "pride of the praise of men" as:

- secret fondness of being noticed
- a love of supremacy
- drawing attention to myself in conversation
- loving to have my name at the top of the list

121

- enjoying flattery
- a forwardness in displaying my talents and attainments publicly, or secretly complimenting myself instead of giving glory to God
- being afraid to launch out for God because I am afraid of what some people might say.

King Saul lost his kingdom because he was afraid of what people thought. Jesus declared that many Pharisees were hell-bound because they tried to please God and the people simultaneously (John 5:41–44; 12:42–43). Paul declared that if he were still seeking to please people, he could not be the servant of Christ (Galatians 1:10). Pleasing people is an insidious form of pride that I seem to fight continually.

5. Am I tempted to promote my church at pastors meetings or church conventions? My mother- and father-in-law had a business conflict arise just before their scheduled departure for a ministry trip to Brazil. At the last minute, they asked if Julie and I were interested in taking their place. We caught up with the traveling pastors, who were all from the same city in Texas, at the airport in Dallas. The leader introduced us as the "Arizona contingent" who would join them in leading revivals on the outskirts of Rio.

Julie and I watched with fascination the unspoken but unmistakable pecking order among these pastors, based entirely upon the size of their churches. At first, the only ones who talked with us were pastors from the smallest churches. During the week, as our church size became known, we were welcomed into conversations with larger and larger groups.

Paul wrote, "We do not dare to classify or compare ourselves with some who commend themselves. When they measure themselves by themselves and compare themselves with themselves, they are not wise" (2 Cor. 10:12).

I hate that stab in my heart when I hear of another's ministry that is better, more meaningful, or more well known than my own. Comparing my ministry and work with others brings heartache, disappointment, and bondage.

6. *Am I feeling shy?* I have often wondered how I survived as a pastor when I struggled continually with shyness. At church parties and functions, I have forced myself to meet people and to encourage the flock. The only clue most folks have had to my bondage was my penchant for isolating myself under the guise of one-on-one counseling or entering into long-winded discussions with a few whenever I was in a group setting.

As I mentioned in an earlier chapter, there is a side of pride that wants to be out front, that delights in being seen and noticed: *I hope everyone notices me and what I say or do. I want the attention.*

But there is a flip side to pride: *Oh my, I feel uncomfortable because people are looking at me. If I am not careful I might call attention to myself, or say something stupid, or do something to embarrass myself, so I will remain quiet and in the background and hope no one notices me.*

I struggle with both sides of pride. I like to be recognized and receive the "pride of the praise of men." On the other hand, my shyness often keeps me from speaking or acting freely, because I fear what people might think.

I used to think God had given me a shy personality. I thought it was my lot in life to struggle with an inferiority complex. Then one day I realized shyness was ruining my personality. A quiet personality is one thing, but shyness is something else. Out of my struggles, I developed a definition of pride: Pride is simply an over-concern with self.

7. Am I content with the gifts, the talents, and the church God has given me? I was leading a conference when a recently retired pastor, well respected and admired in both church and secular circles, invited me to lunch between sessions. I confessed to him my deep-seated struggle with pride. I even recounted how I prayed to be greater than Moses and to do things for God no one else had ever done. He listened intently and smiled knowingly.

The restaurant owners had planted a garden of roses outside. It was spring, and the bushes were covered with bright red Mr. Lincoln roses. Large, pale yellow and pink Peace roses bloomed in abundance. The garden was filled with a sweet aroma. As we stepped outside, my friend mused, "How many *most perfect roses* do you think there are on the earth?"

This is a trick question, I thought, so I didn't answer

quickly. After moments of reflection, I could find no trick, so I said, "Well, I guess there is only one."

"Wouldn't it be a shame," he replied, "if all the other roses ceased to exist because they weren't the one *most perfect?* The world would miss out on a lot of color, sweet fragrance, and enjoyment."

I got the message. Moses and I are no longer in competition. Being the best pastor and doing things for God no one has done no longer fascinate me. The arrogance that fuels those dreams is exorbitant. I would rather corral my pride, pray for humility, and be the pastor God designed me to be.

8

EMPTYING THE RESERVOIR
OF PAIN

SEVERAL YEARS INTO a harried ministry, I began to break down. No mentor had ever explained to me how to handle the stresses of a growing church and a growing family. One Saturday evening I sat behind the orange couch in our den and began to cry. When I got hold of my emotions, I called Steve, our counselor on staff, and said, "I've been crying. I am no psychologist, but I know enough to know I need help."

"I saw this coming," Steve said. "I have contacted a counselor who specializes in management-level stress. His name is Jerry. He is waiting for your call."

During my initial consultation, Jerry gave me a battery of simple tests. He scored the results and said, "I can help you. Ten sessions ought to do it."

I checked with my insurance company and discovered the sessions were not covered in our policy. I told my wife, "I don't think we can afford $500."

She replied, "It will be worth every penny if he can get you fixed for only $500. It's worth that much to stay in the ministry."

I made the investment, and at the end of the third session Jerry said, "One of your tests shows that you are very angry."

Shocked, I said, "How can that be? I'm a pastor.

I'm gentle and kind and tenderhearted and patient."

Jerry said, "I don't know about that, but I do know the test indicates that you are a very angry man. I want you to read *The Angry Book* by Theodore Rubin."[1]

The book was all about me. Rubin's premise is that properly processed anger does not accumulate; however, most people have never learned to handle anger properly. As a result, many build up a large reservoir of unprocessed anger that remains unnoticed until the reservoir overflows.

For about twenty chapters, Rubin details the "anger poisons" that ooze out disguised as anxiety, depression, guilt, over-eating, over-sleeping, over-sexing, over-exercising, over-working, obsessive-compulsive thinking, self-sabotage, bullying, super-sweet talk, insomnia, thinly disguised contempt, exhaustion, and temper explosions. These conspicuous displays can be stand-alone problems, but Rubin conjectures many are the outward manifestations of an inward, unprocessed, overflowing slush fund of anger.

Rubin's book began for me a journey to explore the anger I had accumulated in my soul from the hurts I had experienced in pastoral work. Anger and unresolved hurt can erect barriers between us and God. It was a turning point for me that helped me begin to process the inevitable pain of ministry.

---

[1] Theodore Rubin, *The Angry Book* (New York: Simon & Schuster, Collier Books, 1969).

Weeping with those who weep

I read *The Angry Book* in vain for a clear-cut plan on how to process my anger and to clean out my anger slush fund. Rubin gave helpful suggestions for how to *prevent* a slush fund buildup: For example, I now try to dissipate anger, before it accumulates in my slush fund, by recognizing I am angry, talking about it, and processing it rationally. However, I did not find full relief until Julie and I attended a conference on marital intimacy. God spoke through Dr. David Ferguson about the relationship between hurt and anger. I learned not only why many pastors seethe with unresolved anger but how to heal from past hurts while still on the front lines.

"People get angry because they get hurt," stated Dr. Ferguson. "Think about it: Why do we get angry? People may stand in our way and keep us from getting something we want. Or they say nasty and untrue things about us behind our backs. Or they hurt those we love. There are many ways to get hurt. When we do, we get angry."

Getting hurt is an occupational hazard of pastoring. Sometimes I feel like a marine recruit crawling through the mud while bullets whistle overhead. At any moment, someone in the congregation can lower a machine gun at me and fire. Guns come in various shapes and sizes, and bullets vary in velocity and effect; however, they all have one thing in common: they hurt. One of my primary pastoral goals is to survive.

People shoot at me because I fail to meet their unrealistic or perceived expectations. I was shot at once for saying the wrong thing at a wedding, and I was fired upon (which I deserved!) when I forgot to show up for a wedding. I have been shot for not returning phone calls, for not being evangelistic enough. I have felt the fire for spending too much time with the congregation and not enough with my staff—and vice versa. I stood still while a close friend slid a knife into my side while announcing that I was leading the church away from God and, as a result, he and his family were leaving to find a church with a pastor they could trust.

One morning I raced to cover surgeries at three different hospitals. One was scheduled for six and the other two for six-thirty. At five-fifteen I prayed with a patient at Tucson Medical Center for his six o'clock surgery. Then I drove to El Dorado Hospital and prayed with a woman scheduled for surgery at six-thirty. After that, I ran to my car and raced across town to St. Mary's Hospital, hoping and praying the other six-thirty surgery would be delayed. It was not. I apologized to the family and tried to explain, but the wife would hear no excuse.

"The truth is," she said, "if you were a good pastor, you would have been here."

Her words hurt so badly, I went home and wept.

I've also seen firsthand the hurt felt by pastors' wives. One of our staff counselors gave the Taylor-Johnson Temperament Analysis to our ministerial staff and their spouses. Several weeks later, at a retreat in the White Mountains of Arizona, Steve took each couple aside and shared the results. All things considered, I had normal problems like everyone else.

Then he pulled out my wife's test results and asked Julie, "Have you been raped recently?" She was startled. She thought a moment and said, "No, I'm just a pastor's wife." We spent a long time discussing why her responses fit a pattern called the "rape victim's profile." We struggled to the conclusion that the sense of vulnerability, isolation, and violation that often accompany the pastor's wife role could easily parallel the reactions of a rape victim. (Julie has long since been healed of the hurts of those early years. Now her TJTA results reveal nothing more than normal, everyday problems.)

At that marriage retreat, Dr. Ferguson taught that unprocessed hurt produces tremendous anger. *No wonder I was an angry pastor*, I thought. I looked back over years of enjoyable and fruitful ministry that were mixed with a multitude of unprocessed hurts. Who had time to heal when ministry was so consuming? Besides, even if I had time, I didn't know where to begin.

"Heal the hurts, and you'll heal the anger," explained Dr. Ferguson. "God revealed exactly how to heal our hurts in Matthew 5:4: 'Blessed are those who mourn, for they will be comforted.' Mourning people are people who have been hurt. Hurts are healed by mourning and comforting."

As a pastor, I never felt I was allowed to mourn. I had to be strong for everyone else. Unfortunately, neither did I know how to give comfort.

At a staff retreat in northern Arizona, one of our youth interns began to weep. He was recently married and was departing soon for seminary. He had no job lined up, did not know if he could do the schoolwork, was afraid to leave home, and was questioning God's call. The rest of us felt uncomfortable watching this twenty-four-year-old man come unglued. We tried to encourage him: "Stop crying, Bill, you'll be okay. You're well trained. You will succeed in whatever you decide to do." Someone hollered, "Bill, relax, there are plenty of jobs there. You'll find one!" Another said, "I can think of three reasons why you shouldn't feel this way. . . ."

Nothing helped. Finally, Jennifer, one of our female counselors, shouted, "Would you all shut up! You are not helping him!" At the time I knew she was right but had no idea why.

Now I know: Hurting people do not need advice; they do not need encouragement. They do not need three reasons why they should not feel the way they feel. Hurting people need comfort.

Giving comfort is weeping with those who weep: "I am so sorry they teased you on the bus. I can't imagine how you felt when they were saying those things about you. My heart is filled with sorrow because you were hurt deeply by those kids." It takes emotion to heal emotion, not reasoning, facts, or advice. Comforting words are feeling words that convey love, acceptance, security, and understanding.

It was time for lunch. Dr. Ferguson sent us to the dining room with two instructions: Eat alone with your spouse, and allow your spouse to bring comfort while you mourn an unprocessed hurt. Julie and I found a table alone in the restaurant.

"It's been eighteen years since Jessie died," Julie began. "I've kept my feelings buried for so long." That was true. Julie and I grieved differently after our first-born daughter died. I wanted to talk about Jessie, to look at her pictures, and to savor the good memories, but not Julie. We buried Jessie on a Friday afternoon, and on Monday Julie enrolled in a Master's program at the University of Arizona. She hardly ever mentioned Jessie again.

That afternoon in the restaurant, Julie continued, "I can't tell you how badly it hurt."

She began to cry as the waitress arrived to take our drink orders. The young woman took one look at my weeping wife and quickly turned away. The depth of Julie's emotions shocked me. I had no idea she hurt so badly.

I followed Dr. Ferguson's suggestions: "Julie, I am so sorry you feel like this. I know it hurts. I can't imagine your feelings as a mother watching your first-born die in your arms."

Then she really began to cry. The waitress returned, and I gently motioned her away. She nodded and left.

Julie wept for twenty minutes. When she settled down, I asked, "Why don't I sit here and let you tell me how much it hurt." So she did. For over an hour, she detailed the hurts, the unfulfilled dreams, the feelings of failure and guilt that come with the death of a child. We never got lunch. Instead, we got something better: Julie began to heal.

Forgiveness for a tub of hurt

The same principles are at work in healing from painful ministry wounds. Unfortunately, when I am wounded in ministry, I never have the luxury of going behind the lines to get well. Every other day seems like Sunday. People need counseling, and problems need solving. Couples keep falling in love and wanting to get married, and somebody always seems to be dying. Failing marriages need strengthening, and angry people need soothing. Bible classes need teaching. Elders need presentations. I find it impossible to call a halt every time I need to lick my wounds and heal my hurts.

The only option, besides bailing out of ministry, is to process the hurt and anger while still serving others in ministry. I've developed a model for healing when I am unable to withdraw to lick my wounds:

First, I find someone safe who knows how to comfort. Few things are more frustrating than to pour out my heart to someone who does not know how to comfort. I find bringing emotions and feelings to the surface difficult. I want to know that the people to whom I reveal my pain will not look at me blankly and wonder what to say, so that I wish I had never said anything. When I mourn with people who do not know how to comfort, I suffer a double hurt: I feel bad because I suffer the deep-seated hurts all over again, and I hurt because the pain I brought up does not go away. I need people who know how to put their arms around me and weep when I weep—as well as rejoice when I rejoice. Of course, the process must be reciprocated if the relationship is to flourish.

It takes time to cultivate safe, trustworthy relationships, but the investment must be made if the hurts are to be healed. The only two females I open up to are my wife and a spiritual woman in our congregation who is old enough to be my mother. The other five are men.

Second, I identify hurt and anger as soon as possible. When I feel angry, I analyze where I have been disappointed or hurt. A hurt lurks behind every anger. I want to process my hurts before they get buried. When painful hurts arise in my mind, I try to pause to process them, trying to feel their hurt. I find it useful to sit quietly and pray for God to bring to mind those long ago, unhealed hurts that lie just below the surface of my subconscious.

Third, I mourn the hurts and allow my comforter to comfort. Crying and expressing verbally how much I hurt used to be hard for me—especially in front of someone. However, since I have been working to do this, mourning like Jesus recommended feels too good, and accomplishes too much, to keep my hurt and anger bottled up inside.

Sometimes when I am wounded I call my next-door neighbor, Pete, and invite myself over. We sit in his living room while I pour out how I feel and what went through my mind when someone hurt me with their words; I reveal what I wanted to say but did not. Pete is a sensitive Christian man who knows how to comfort.

Jesus said, "It is more blessed to give than to receive." Like many pastors, I find it hard to receive. I have learned how to give, because giving is a built-in necessity of ministry. However, I have to work at receiving. It feels awkward to ask someone to listen to my hurts and comfort me so I can heal. However, no one has ever refused. People seem honored to be asked. So I receive the comfort and thank them for it, and praise God for the healing process.

Fourth, I close the loop through confession and forgiveness. I learned about the importance of this when I was young, foolish, and newly married. I labored in my first full-time pastorate for three years without a day off. I had a church to build and people to reach. One Monday Julie suggested we take an overnight trip to Phoenix, about one hundred miles north of Tucson. I told her that if I worked hard I could get my sermon done early, and we could depart by noon on Friday. So the trip was planned and the hotel reservation made for our much-needed mini-vacation.

At 11:45 A.M. on Friday, my phone rang. Kyle, one of my deacons, had heard that Julie and I were driving to Phoenix. The repair shop had just called to tell him that his car, which had broken down in Phoenix the previous weekend, was ready to be picked up.

"Could you give me a ride to Phoenix?" he asked. "The repair shop is near the interstate."

I had no choice: How would it look for the pastor to refuse aid to a deacon in distress?

I picked up the phone and called Julie: "I'll be home and ready to go at noon. Oh, by the way, Kyle called and needs a ride to Phoenix to pick up his car. You don't mind, do you?" The silence was deafening. Click. She hung up on me.

I hurried home, loaded the suitcases into the trunk, and opened the front passenger door for Julie. She refused to get in. She opened the back door and slid into the seat, as I said, "Oh no, Julie, Kyle can ride in the back. He'll understand."

"No. He can sit in the front with you."

Julie cried all the way to Phoenix. I know, because I kept looking in the rearview mirror. She never spoke to Kyle or to me. In fact, she hardly said a word the entire trip. Late Saturday afternoon, back in Tucson, I opened the trunk to unload our suitcases and said the only thing that seemed appropriate. "Look, if you want a divorce, it's all right with me."

She looked me hard in the eye and replied, "Divorce is not an option. We will work this out."

Realizing I had hurt her, I apologized profusely.

She told me she forgave me and not to worry about it. Deep inside I knew she still hurt, but I had no idea of the depth of her hurt.

Over the years I brought up the Phoenix trip several times: "I don't feel like we really settled that issue. Will you forgive me for what I did that weekend? Please?"

She said on every occasion, "Yes, I forgive you." But I knew the wound was not healed.

My perspective was that Julie had about a "quart-sized bottle's worth" of pain. So I showed up occasionally and asked for about a quart-sized bottle's worth of forgiveness. Unfortunately, she was carrying about a ten-gallon tub of hurt. It was hard for Julie to forgive a lot of hurt when I was asking for only a little bit of forgiveness.

One day I said to Julie, "Sweetheart, I really want to talk about the hurt and pain of our trip to Phoenix. I want you to take however long you need to tell me about your feelings of hurt, betrayal, rejection, sadness, fear, and aloneness. I want to hear how badly I hurt you."

It was like I gave her a gun and said, "Shoot me." So she did.

"I felt deeply betrayed," she began. "I feared for what our future would be like. I wondered if you really did love me at all. I was terrified I would spend the rest of my marriage in loneliness. I felt so neglected. I tried to imagine what I had done to deserve such rejection."

The more she shared her pain, the more I understood how deeply I had hurt her. Then I began to cry as I felt for the first time the agony I had put her through. Finally, I asked one more time, "I am so sorry, will you forgive me?"

For the first time, I made a request for forgiveness based upon a true understanding of her pain. Through tears, Julie said, "Yes, I forgive you." The hurt was healed. I have never again felt the need to ask her forgiveness for the Phoenix trip.

A ten-gallon tub of hurt requires a ten-gallon tub of understanding and forgiveness. That is the final key to healing from pastoral hurts while remaining to fight on the front lines for Jesus Christ.

9

MOURNING UNTIL
FORGIVENESS COMES

I LIVED THROUGH an attack that took a full year off my life. I used to tell people somewhat facetiously that I planned to live until I was eighty-five. I intended to preach twice on Sunday, play golf on Monday, and die quietly in my sleep before dawn on Tuesday. Now I tell them I'll be lucky to make it to eighty-four. The stress and anxiety produced by one personal attack from someone at church cut off at least twelve months of my life.

The attack was already underway the day I listened in disbelief as one of our elders relayed a message that he said came from a powerful church member: "He said that he will destroy you. He will get your picture on the front page of the Sunday newspaper and destroy you. He said that you will never preach in a Southern Baptist Church, or in any other church, again!"

This was no idle threat. The person I believed was behind the warning had the power and the contacts to get me on the front page of the paper. This person demanded we close our newly constituted deliverance ministry. This ministry operated under the umbrella of the church counseling department and provided such services as prayer therapy for those exposed to occultic activity, discipleship training in spiritual warfare in accordance with Ephesians 6:10–17 and 1 John 2:10–12, occasional direct confrontations for people suffering with demonic problems, and cleansing prayers for places and objects that may have had occultic contamination.

This particular member had encountered the ministry and did not like what he saw. I believe he decided it was theologically inconsistent with our church polity and that it was his responsibility to remove it. He held several trump cards that threatened the ministry's existence, held out the possibility of a church split, and could potentially discredit my ministry. The first card was that few, even among our church leaders, knew of the existence of our spiritual-warfare endeavors. I assume he figured that if our members knew we were helping people with demonic problems, they would be confused or frightened. The reason our deliverance ministry operated quietly, especially during its infancy, was that just as we never talked openly about someone's marital problems, neither did we discuss in public someone's demonic problems.

The most miserable night of my life, next to the night my daughter was born with birth defects, was the night that trump card was played. Before our church elders, I was accused, along with others in the deliverance ministry, not only of having a deliverance ministry but of biblical inconsistencies and thus abuse. I was so shocked at being accused of heresy and described as a "misguided, religious fanatic" that I could not speak in my defense. At 11:00 P.M., when the meeting ended, I went home and wept. The fear of a church split and my forced termination paralyzed me. I was so shaken I wondered whether I might be guilty of the charges.

Julie awakened to find me crying.

"The issue is in the hands of the elders now," she said. "If you have cultivated them well, you will be all right."

I wondered whether the years of weekly discipleship classes, meetings, lunches, and shared ministry with my elders were about to pay off. Julie was right; the situation was out of my hands. But I didn't sleep that night.

When the newspaper arrived at 5:15 the next morning, I turned quickly to the classified section and began searching for a new job. Slowly it dawned on me that I was qualified to do little in the marketplace. Not many jobs call for college degrees in Greek and religion. My thinking tumbled out of control. Even if I were not fired, the church would be devastated, split down the middle.

Shortly thereafter I was disturbed by a knock at the door. Bad news travels quickly. Our children's minister had come with a word of encouragement. "The fact that the battle gets rough is no reason to quit or back down," he said. "Much is at stake. Many people need what our deliverance ministry has to offer. You are on the right track. Don't back down. We are with you."

Easy for him to say, I thought.

Trumped again

In the next few weeks the elders held fast. They did not ask me to resign. After many hours of discussion, we voted to continue learning about spiritual warfare and developing a strong deliverance ministry. I am glad I did not have to make this decision alone.

But soon the next card was played. Through a series of circumstances, the elders were forced to take a key issue in the dispute to the church for a vote.

I was astounded, though, when only ninety people (out of about three thousand) bothered to attend the business meeting. The church split I feared never materialized. As a result of the vote, eighteen people left the church; that hardly qualified as a split. None of my fears transpired like I imagined. About this time my brother-in-law passed along to me one of his favorite sayings. I liked it so much I recorded it in the front of my Bible: "Nothing is ever as good or as bad as you think it is."

While my worst fears were never realized, the attack seemed relentless. Several weeks after the vote, I got my first call from a newspaper reporter. He asked all sorts of questions about our church, about demons, exorcisms, and our deliverance ministry. The third time the reporter called, he asked why I was reluctant to answer his questions.

"I don't need the publicity," I said. "I have no control over what you'll write or over which comments you'll include and what context you'll put them in." He never called me again.

But feelings of anger and hatred began oozing into my consciousness. Hatred filled my heart. I knew the importance of forgiveness, but I hurt so badly, I could not bring myself to say the word "forgiveness," much less do it.

One morning I sat in my car in a hospital parking lot and tried to empty before God a heart filled with anger and hurt. The sick parishioner inside the hospital would wait until later. I opened my Bible to David's imprecatory psalms and sought peace as I read how the sweet singer of Israel prayed for God to bring down disease, destruction, and despair upon his enemies. Expressing my anger and calling out for vengeance brought momentary release, though I found no long-term satisfaction in the exercise. I had not yet discovered the biblical principle that the only sure way to empty the hurt and anger seething in my cup was to mourn my hurt with someone who knew how to comfort.

I have purposely not related many details of this story. Telling one side without the other is not fair. I resist attempting to attribute motives to others, but the attack by my adversary seemed to be motivated, at least partially, by pain. I believe he got hurt—a lot. He was likely wounded by the actions of some on our deliverance team. He was hurt by the rebuff by our elders when he demanded a hearing but didn't get one. I am certain he was wounded when I misinterpreted the flag of truce he waved early on to settle the issue. He wanted to meet with me. I chose to let others go in my place. I am sorry he was wounded, too.

Whenever people attack me or gossip about me or try to undermine my ministry, it is easy to blame their fallen nature and respond by raising defenses and fending off the onslaught. However, a better model exists. Hurt lurks behind anger. Why were they so angry with me? Because somewhere along the line, I hurt them. Why do people say those nasty things about me? Because I disappointed them, or someone close to them, and they got hurt. Angry behavior is a direct result of their hurt. The best way to diffuse anger and personal attack is to discern how your enemy was wounded and proceed to heal the hurt. A heart to heart discussion of the hurt, how it occurred, and a deeply felt apology can defuse most personal attacks. But I did not know that then.

Prerequisite to forgiveness

For three months I awakened early every Sunday to check the front page of the newspaper but found nothing there. Finally I set aside the threats as idle. The following Sunday I did not bother to check the paper before driving to church. As I opened the door, the first person I encountered held up the front page of the Sunday paper: "Have you seen this?"

The publisher had used an old file photo of me, in happier times, from the newspaper archives. The big smile on my face looked incongruous with the negative comments from local pastors criticizing and making fun of our church and me. I was so traumatized that I didn't stop to read the article. I determined my best course of action was to ignore the front page until I had time to develop a proper response. I preached that morning and went home to lick my wounds.

Later, in the quiet of my room, I pored over every word in the article. I had to admit the reporter had done a fair and accurate job of reporting. While not as bad as I had imagined it would be, the article did report on our spiritual-warfare ministry. I knew fallout was soon to come.

Late that afternoon one of our ministers relayed a reported message from my foe: "They will be lined up outside Roger's door on Monday morning demanding his resignation."

The next morning when I came to the office, Gary Shrader, our missions pastor, gave me perhaps the best bit of advice I have ever received. "Right now," he said, "is the time when the average pastor does something really stupid."

I waited for him to continue, but there was no more to come. Then I understood the message had been delivered. I blurted to him, "The pressure is so great I want to quit and resign—but that would be stupid. Also, I want to stand in the pulpit next Sunday and blast my rival and tell everyone what he's been doing behind the scenes—but that would be stupid."

The next Sunday Steve Dowdle—who was overseeing both our counseling and deliverance ministries—

and I together delivered the Sunday morning message. We called attention to the previous Sunday's front-page article. I spent the first half of the sermon explaining the theological underpinnings of spiritual warfare. Steve then described the processes, both psychological and spiritual, that we used to help people who struggled with the occult. The response was overwhelmingly positive.

No one lined up outside my door to demand my resignation. Instead, I received calls and letters from people and pastors who were excited that someone was willing to stand against the Evil One. My favorite word of assurance came from a retired marine general who read the article and invited me to play golf. When we finished he said, "I suppose you are wondering why I asked you to play. I read the article, and a friend from your church filled me in on what really happened. I just wanted to meet a pastor who's been through the fire and survived."

A friend surveyed the scene and observed, "This reminds me of when Joseph dined with his brothers and announced, 'You meant this for evil; but God meant it for good.'"

The support blunted the agony but did not take away the dull ache in my heart. I told God I forgave my offender, but I knew that I was lying. I never wanted to see my antagonist again. I fantasized terrible things. I imagined that one day he was in hell and called out for water. God asked me to take to him a drop on my fingertip. Slowly I shook my head and said no.

While the conflict subsided, I harbored for years an unforgiving spirit of bitterness toward this man. It became increasingly difficult to hear from God in prayer, and especially to interact with him when I worked on my sermons. My quiet times were distracted, and the joy and peace of the Spirit seemed further away than I ever imagined possible. I tried to tap in to the forgiveness God gave in Christ and extend it to my enemy.

I thought I had finally forgiven him, until one night I dreamed I was serving in the armed forces in World War II as an army lieutenant. We had captured a platoon of German soldiers, and one of my men asked if we could shoot them. I was shocked at the diabolical suggestion. "Of course not," I replied. "We are Americans; we don't shoot prisoners." Just then one of the captured German officers turned and, in my dream, I recognized my adversary.

Instantly I cried, "Shoot him! Shoot him! Shoot him!"

I awakened in a cold sweat to hear Julie shouting, "Roger, Roger, wake up, wake up! You're having a bad dream!" I shook as I related to her the dream and the feelings it evoked.

"I can't believe it has been over ten years," I said. "I still have such deep emotions buried inside. I thought I had forgiven him a long time ago." So once more I prayed and tried to forgive this person for the pain he had caused. In bed, at 3:00 A.M., Julie allowed me to do what Jesus spoke of in Matthew 5:4: "Blessed are those who mourn, for they will be comforted."

"Why don't you tell me how much he hurt you?" she began. So I did. She knew which questions to ask: "How did it feel when you realized you had been betrayed? What was it like to sit up all night thinking you were soon to be fired? Describe the trauma you experienced at the elder meeting the night you faced your accusers. How did you feel when two of your closest friends turned their backs on you? What was it like to go to the denominational leaders for help and feel like you were rebuffed?"

I began to mourn, and Julie began to comfort me: "I am so sorry for the things that happened to you," she said. "I know it hurt more than words can describe when you saw yourself on the front page of the Sunday paper. My heart grieves for the sorrow you endured at losing church members over this issue. I know you felt like a failure."

When the tearful process finally concluded that evening, I was ready to forgive him. And I did.

Recently I ran into the gentleman and his wife at the mall. I had no inclination to turn and walk the other way. We smiled, shook hands, and talked like any two civilized adults about families and health. Perhaps someday we will open the door to the past and do some healing together. Perhaps not. But I know that while he may not be my best friend in heaven, we will both be there, saved by the grace of our Lord Jesus Christ.

10

GOD AMONG THE DOUBTS

THE ROOM FULL OF MINISTERS hushed when I asked, "Is there anyone here who has never once doubted the reality and truth of Christianity?"

One minister raised his hand.

"Do you mean to tell me that you have never once," I pressed, "in all of your life had at least one small doubt that Christianity might not be true?"

"That's right," he replied. "I have never had a single doubt—not one."

I thought to myself that he was either a dullard or a liar but thought better of enunciating my thoughts. I gave some innocuous response and continued leading the prayer time. Later, as I reflected on his remark, I considered that a third option probably existed. Perhaps it was possible for someone to have such simple, childlike faith that doubts never occurred. I would not know. I am not one of those persons.

My wife, Julie, might be one.

"Why do you ask so many questions?" she often asks. "Why can't you just accept the Bible at face value and believe it?"

"It is not that simple," I reply.

Once upon a time it was. I became a Christian with childlike faith at the age of seven. Nary a doubt entered my mind. Questions regarding the validity of Christianity arose during my senior year in high school when a friend gave me a Roman Catholic *Douay Version* of the Bible. No other version, except the venerated and difficult-to-understand King James, had ever graced my fingertips. I now held in my hands the first easy-to-read English version I had seen. I decided to read it straight through before I graduated in May.

My struggles commenced with the opening chapters of Genesis. I suppose I had never before read Genesis carefully in the King James Version. My quandary began that night in bed when I realized God had not created the sun until day four. It bothered me that God made light and darkness on day one and separated the sky from the waters on day two and created dry land and vegetation on day three—but did not get around to the sun, moon, and the stars until day four. How could the earth have light before it had a sun?

Furthermore, it bothered me that chlorophyll-producing green plants thrived before a sun existed to power them. My racing mind slowed when I reasoned that new plants could surely live for twenty-four hours until God got around to making the sun. I read how God made the birds and the sea creatures on day five and fashioned land animals and man on day six. Then I went to sleep.

The next night I discovered a direct contradiction: Moses declared in Genesis 2 that no shrub existed and no plant had sprung up when God formed man out of dust and breathed into his nostrils the breath of life. Did Moses forget what he had just written? In chapter 1 he said that plants were created three days before man. In chapter 2, he emphatically declared that no plants existed when God scooped up dust to fashion a body for man. *What gives?* I thought.

Since my childhood faith was strong, it did not take much to settle my high school musings. Alfred Rehwinkel's *The Flood* brought comfort that brilliant men had figured out explanations for all sorts of complex interfaces between the Bible and science.[1]

I could live off their faith.

Disillusioning discoveries

My faith held strong through college and into my early pastoral career. Then, while riding a bus on a high school mission tour from Arizona to Oregon, I read *The Red Limit* by Timothy Ferris.[2] This astronomical survey of the universe from the Big Bang to the present was mind-boggling. During the first three minutes after Creation, hundreds of subatomic particles came into being, including protons, neutrons, and electrons, which coalesced into hydrogen, helium, and a few lithium nuclei. After three minutes, not enough heat energy remained to fuse any heavier elements.

Ferris demonstrated how gravity coalesced large clouds of hydrogen and helium gas over long periods of time for the making of stars and galaxies. In short,

[1] Alfred Rehwinkel, *The Flood* (St. Louis, Mo.: Concordia Publishing House, 1966).
[2] Timothy Ferris, *The Red Limit* (New York: Bantam Books, 1979).

Ferris's intricate explanation of how every element heavier than helium is produced either during nuclear fusion inside a star or an explosion during the star's demise had dramatic implications! The idea that the "dust of the earth" used by God to create Adam was cooked up inside an exploded star somewhere out in the universe conflicted dramatically with my youthful understanding that one day, about six thousand years ago, God created the heavens and the earth.

I was disillusioned to discover from Ferris that countless stars had burst into existence, lived a full life, and expired before our own sun was created about four-and-a-half billion years ago. I was shocked to discover how insignificant our sun is in the galaxy. We are four-fifths of the way out toward the edge of the Milky Way in a trough between the Sagittarius and Orion arms. My faith shook as it dawned on me that the physics of star formation demanded the creation of a solar system of planets around every star (now increasingly verified by astronomical observation). The very idea that life might exist on some planet elsewhere in the universe rocked my secure biblical foundations:

How would God relate to other life in the universe?

Could there be other fallen races?

Did Jesus die for people somewhere else, too?

Would "the Lamb slain *before the foundation of the cosmos*" take on more meaning than I ever imagined? (Much later I discovered that C. S. Lewis had considered all these issues in his *Space Trilogy* before I was born!)

The barren desert landscape outside the bus window just south of Las Vegas looked much like the inside of my heart. The more I read, the less I believed in a God who was big enough to oversee the whole universe. Maybe God really was a created figment of man's hope-filled imagination. If he did exist, how could he be everywhere all the time in a universe so immense? Earth was not the center of anything. How could he have time for us? How could man be made of stardust?

My original doubts flooded back with a vengeance.

When we returned home, I decided to squelch my uncertainties and follow Asaph's model in Psalm 73 for handling doubts. The poet almost lost his faith when he contemplated the apparent earthly success of the ungodly as compared to the godly. He concluded, "If I had said, 'I will speak thus [of all my doubts],' I would have betrayed . . . your children" (v. 15). Asaph determined that when there was a mist in the pulpit, there would surely be fog in the pews. I vowed to keep my reservations to myself. A doubting preacher can bring mass confusion to the flock.

Several pastors and I once discussed the fall from grace of a nationally known pastor. His ministry thrived up to the moment when his immoral actions were exposed.

"How could God bless this man's work and ministry while he lived a life of hypocrisy and deceit?" we all wondered.

"God never promised to honor the preacher," one friend reasoned; "but he has promised always to honor his Word."

"We must never back down from preaching the Word just because we cannot live up to it all," said another. "If we wait until we've mastered all the truths in a passage, many texts will remain forever unpreached."

Trying to simplify the discussion, I added, "I can't postpone preaching on gluttony until I control my weight. Gluttony is a sin no matter how much I weigh."

Therefore, I vowed to preach God's Word carefully and faithfully while I worked through my confusions.

Winding faith

But I couldn't ignore my internal struggle. In my spare time, I resolved to study astral physics and quantum mechanics until I could reconcile the Bible and science. I started with Einstein's theories and read books like *Einstein's Universe* by Nigel Calder, *Relativity Visualized* by Lewis Epstein, and *A Brief History of Time* by Stephen Hawking, until I could explain in simple terms how massive bodies warp space-time, how the universe works, and why time stops at the event horizon of a black hole. The concept of eternity was easy to accept when I realized observable places exist in the universe where time actually does stand still.

I studied quantum mechanics and read books like *Taking the Quantum Leap* by Fred Wolf and *The First Three Minutes* by Steven Weinberg. I discovered that physics on the subatomic level determined the structure of everything on the macro level. I learned that the universe exists in multiple dimensions—most probably six small ones that rolled up at the moment of Creation and the four that we discern easily in everyday life: length, width, and height, plus time.

Since math is the language of physics, I studied several books on mathematics, like *One Two Three—Infinity* by George Gamow, and learned that the mathematical models of multidimensional space predict that everything in the universe becomes a single point when passing through eleven spatial dimensions. This revelation, plus the implications of warped space-time, forever settled my mind as to how God could be omnipresent in an enormous, expanding universe.

I resolved to study enough anthropology to get a feel for the creation of man. *Lucy*, by Donald Johanson and Maitland Edey, provided me with a broad, sweeping overview of the "emergence" of mankind on earth. Lucy is a fossilized, three-foot-tall female creature who walked the savannas of Africa 3 million years ago. Lucy was not human, nor was she ape, chimpanzee, or monkey. I understood how prehistoric Lucy might fit within the context of any of the Christian-based theories of Adamic creation.

My faith was bolstered in the biological arena

when *The Search for Eve* by Michael Brown was published. This scholarly work, based on years of careful research on human mitochondria from people groups all over the world, demonstrated beyond the shadow of a doubt that every human being alive today had one common female ancestor. Scientific proof for the existence of Eve further sustained my faith.

I studied geology in order to satisfy my mind that geologists had valid reasons for dating rocks back into the millions and billions of years old. I also read the works of Christians who attempted to reconcile the apparent contradiction between science and Scripture by postulating a "mature earth" theory—that God created the universe with fossils and stars that just looked millions and billions of years old, when they were actually created just thousands of years prior. Though the idea that God played tricks in Creation was untenable to me, I admired the honest attempt to solve the apparent disharmony.

Preaching with doubt

But this long search—and long periods of unresolved doubt—stole my joy, sapped my strength, and affected the faith of those around me. I wish I had lived with more faith during those years. I remember preaching funerals while wondering if there was life after death. Preaching with power about the miracles in Scripture while pondering their validity produced guilt. However, I never dipped into unbelieving despair. I never preached things I did not believe.

Not surprisingly, relief came from the Bible. What-ever the Creation accounts in Genesis meant, there was no confusion as to the meaning of Hebrews 11:3: "By faith we understand that the universe was formed at God's command, so that what is seen was not made out of what was visible."

How did the writer to the Hebrews know in the first century what it took science nineteen hundred years more to discover? I concluded God must have told him.

While both twentieth-century science and the Bible agree that the universe exploded into existence at a single point out of absolutely nothing, I finally concluded that God did not reveal enough for us to solve all the riddles of science and the Bible. The truth probably lies somewhere on the compendium between the two extremes of naturalistic materialism, which hypothesizes that the universe and life evolved over time by chance because there is no God, and scientific creationism, which, in its most extreme form, main-tains a strict belief in seven twenty-four-hour days of creation about six thousand years ago.

I made peace with my doubts when I concluded that the main issue of faith is not deciphering the facts of Creation but settling the issue of the resurrec-tion of Jesus Christ. I could not reconcile Genesis 1 and 2 just yet, but I could trust my life to the One who cheated death and promised that if I believed in him, I, too, could cheat death and live forever. I concluded Paul had the right perspective. In an attempt to convert the Athenians in Acts 17:16–31, Paul mentioned the God who created heaven and earth, but he planted his arguments firmly in the fact that Jesus Christ was not in the tomb on Easter morning. I decided to anchor my faith likewise.

The answer to unbelief resided in a choice of my will. It was my choice to believe the Scriptures—or not. My faith could not rest on feelings or emotions. Faith could not depend on my ability to figure everything out. Mark Twain said, "It is not what I don't understand about the Bible that bothers me, but what I do understand." I understood enough to believe. The rest would have to take care of itself.

I never sensed that God punished me for my doubts. I never once had the impression that he was angry with my unbelief—disappointed perhaps, but not irate. I sensed all along that he lovingly supported my searching and stood unflinchingly by my side. Never once did I feel betrayed or deserted. He knew I would work through my struggles. Perhaps he considered my life and ministry worth saving.

I was living in faith when I encountered a little known book in the Christian community—*The Meaning of Creation* by Conrad Hyers.[3] Hyers' premise for unpacking the Genesis Creation is based on understanding Hebrew poetry.

English poets tend to rhyme words: "Hickory,

---

[3]Conrad Hyers, *The Meaning of Creation* (Atlanta: John Knox Press, 1984).

dickory, dock, the mouse ran up the clock." Hebrew poets rhymed thoughts by writing a phrase and then repeating it with a slight twist of wording or meaning. The poet says something and then recapitulates with other expressions—like I just did. This is why Hebrew wisdom literature is often redundant and occasionally confusing. For example, Jesus was not really riding three different animals on Palm Sunday, as Matthew indicates. Matthew was quoting verbatim Zechariah's prophetical, poetical rhyming of "colt" with "donkey" and "ass."

According to Hyers, Moses never intended Genesis to be a scientific dissertation on Creation. In fact, according to Hyers, Moses would be both startled and confused at the biblical debates that swirl around science today. The issue for Moses was not science and the Bible. He wanted to know: Who is the real God? Elohim of the Israelites? Or the myriad gods of the Egyptians? With each day of the Creation, Moses systematically declared, "My God is bigger than your god," as he demonstrated that the Egyptian "gods" were not gods at all. They were all creations of Elohim! When he demonstrated the intricate rhyming schemes of Genesis 1, like how day one rhymes with day four, and two with five, and three with six, I was convinced!

Reading *The Meaning of Creation* strengthened my faith, which had already begun to grow, though I wish now I had read it in high school. Simple faith is preferable to raging doubts, but my protracted, intense struggles produced a stronger faith. Simple, unwavering childlike faith is lovely to behold. But so is complex, hard-earned faith that has taken years to formulate and resolve.

Santa Claus faith

I have worked for almost ten years to relocate our church from a small, landlocked corner to a much larger tract of land. The move will soon be completed, but not without a price. I understand now why nearly 50 percent of pastors change churches within two years after a major church building project. Nothing came in under budget. Change orders constantly increased the price. Plans were never ready on time. The subcontractors were late.

And then the kicker: Would the people keep giving? As we neared the end of the project, the finances got squeezed. We arranged to complete the project without selling our old site; however, we knew that if it sold, our financial stress would disappear.

One day, immersed in prayer, I sensed God speak deep within. *Stop worrying,* he said, *the site will sell. I promise. All will be well. You need your strength for other things.*

I recorded my prayer and God's assurance in my journal and lived for several months in peace. Then a new round of cost increases shattered my well-being and faith. *What if I just made all that up?* I thought to myself. *What if God never spoke to me and I am just deluding myself?*

I began to worry again.

About this time, Julie and I were trying to sell a car. We didn't really have to sell it, but it seemed like time for a change. Since we had gone three weeks without an offer, we were making plans to keep it. On Saturday morning, the twenty-first day the ad had been in the paper, I sat down with God to pray. I was rather stressed out concerning the relocation finances and told God so.

God spoke to me: *Didn't I tell you the old property would sell? Don't you believe me? I told you to relax and stop worrying.*

"But God, what if it really wasn't you? I think I'm going to keep worrying because I am really stressed out about this."

All will be fine. In fact, I will give you a sign to help you relax. Your car will sell today.

I had to be imagining this. There was no way the car would sell that day. I wasn't even planning to be around all day. I was going to play golf, and then head to the mall to shop with the children. I would be at church the next day from seven until one; then I would leave for the airport at one-fifteen to catch a flight to Tulsa. The car could not sell this weekend.

"Oh, come on, God," I said as I stood, "I am making all this up."

That evening, at seven-thirty, I listened to our phone answering machine. A couple had called about the car. "I am returning your call about my car," I said as they answered the phone.

"We want to come see it."

"Well, it's dark now . . . and . . . I really don't have time to show it to you . . . and my wife and I have pretty much decided to keep it."

"We really do want to come see it tonight."

So, at eight-fifteen, the gentleman and his wife arrived from across town. "Is this the one?" he asked, peering at the car parked close to the street. He opened the door and slowly looked around inside. "The paper said you were asking $7,200. I'll give you $7,000 right now, on the spot."

"Wait a minute," I said. "You can't buy a car in the dark. You can't even see the finish, or the tires; you haven't even looked under the hood."

"We have another car just like this one, and we love it. We'll take it."

I grew stubborn: "I am not going to sell you a car you haven't even driven. I'll tell you what, I'll slip out of church a little early tomorrow and be here just before one o'clock. You be here, ready to go, and we'll drive around the block. I have to leave for the airport at one-fifteen. If you still want it after you drive it, it's yours."

They were waiting in my driveway when I got home from church. Shortly before I left for the airport, we shook hands on the deal; my car was gone.

Five weeks later we shook hands on a deal to sell our old site, just as God had said.

I began asking myself how many burning bushes it was going to take? One should be enough. It was time I made a consious choice of my will to believe.

Recently, by choice, I have resolved to believe in God like I used to believe in Santa Claus. Of course, Santa has nothing to substantiate his existence. God has given thousands of verifiable signs and proofs. I long ago put away my belief in Santa, but I have never forgotten the sense of complete, childlike, unquestioning abandonment of faith I had in him. Now that I am an adult, I want to enjoy that same sense of unquestioning belief in God.

Recently one of our church secretaries was having heart trouble. Irregular heartbeats had gone on too long. Neither electric shock nor medication restored sinus rhythm. Medical options were exhausted. One person requested prayer for her healing during our weekly Wednesday morning staff prayer meeting.

"God can handle this," I said. "Let's just believe God like when we were little children believing in Santa Claus. He loves simple, childlike faith. Let's ask God to heal her heart and restore the right rhythms." I was not at all surprised when, later that day, her heart returned to good rhythm. I believe with all of my heart in a Creator God who delights to honor the prayers and faith of those who believe him—whether they struggle or not.